Authentic Indian Cooking
with Your Instant Pot®

Classic and Innovative Recipes
for the Home Cook

Vasanti Bhadkamkar-Balan

creator of Signature Concoctions

PAGE STREET
PUBLISHING CO.

PAGE STREET
PUBLISHING CO.

First published in 2021 by
Page Street Publishing Co.
27 Congress Street, Suite 105
Salem, MA 01970
www.pagestreetpublishing.com

Distributed by Macmillan, sales in Canada by The Canadian Manda Group.

25   24   23   22   21   1   2   3   4   5

ISBN-13: 978-1-64567-404-7
ISBN-10: 1-645-67404-5

Library of Congress Control Number: 2021931370

Cover and book design by Molly Kate Young for Page Street Publishing Co.
Photography by Vasanti Bhadkamkar-Balan

Printed and bound in China

Instant Pot® is a registered trademark of Double Insight, Inc., which was not involved in the creation of this book.

My Happy Family

Contents

For Meat and
Poultry *Lovers*

My husband is a meat lover and cannot go without it for more than a day, so it's safe to say I've had a lot of practice preparing everything from chicken to beef and from pork to lamb. I enjoy the process of creating new recipes and have included some of my favorites in this chapter, like Pudina Gosht (Minty Lamb Curry; page 18) and Methi Murgh Handi (Fenugreek Chicken Curry; page 27). I also love to put my own spin on classics, like the Maharashtrian Pandhra Rassa (Chicken in Mild Coconut Curry; page 36). Over the years, I have also perfected the recipe for the restaurant favorite Chicken Tikka Masala (Chicken in Creamy Tomato Sauce; page 12). I've held on to family recipes, like the Ball Curry (Meatball Curry; page 15), which I learned from my mother-in-law so I could make my husband his favorite curry. I'm sharing my take on some of the popular dishes from different regions in India, like the North Indian Murgh Malaiwala (Chicken in Herbed Cream Sauce; page 21), Maharashtrian Lamb Kala Masala (Lamb in Onion-Coconut Curry; page 24), Rajasthani Laal Maas (Lamb in Red Curry; page 30) and the Keralan Beef Ularthiyathu (Beef Roast; page 33).

The delicious curries in this chapter are traditionally made with a lot of sautéing and stirring before they are simmered away for hours on the stove so that the meat is cooked to tender, melt-in-your-mouth perfection. Thanks to the Instant Pot, these time-consuming recipes can be made in less than half the time, yet they have the same depth of flavor and the meat is soft, succulent and falling off the bone.

All the dishes in this chapter are typically served as a main course and pair very well with steamed basmati rice and Indian breads like naan, rotis or parathas.

Chicken Tikka Masala

(Chicken in Creamy Tomato Sauce)

This is one of the most popular dishes of Indian cuisine and is on the menu of almost every Indian restaurant in the world! I love its robust and smoky flavor, which comes from adding the tandoor-grilled chicken tikka pieces to the tomato-cream masala sauce.

While you can find hundreds of recipes for making this dish in the Instant Pot, my recipe is truly unique! I cook the marinated chicken in a steamer basket with the sauce at the bottom in the main pot. This process allows the marinade to drip into the sauce, enhancing its flavor. The cooked chicken pieces are broiled and then added to the sauce. The dish is finished off with heavy cream and kasuri methi (dried fenugreek).

Serves 4

Marinade

½ cup (120 ml) plain, unsweetened Greek yogurt

2 cloves garlic, finely grated

½-inch (1.3-cm) piece fresh ginger, finely grated

1 tbsp (6 g) Kashmiri red chili powder (see Notes)

Red chili powder, as needed

1 tsp Easy Garam Masala (page 172)

1 tbsp (15 ml) mustard oil or neutral oil of choice

Salt, as needed

2 lb (908 g) boneless, skinless chicken thighs, cut into 1½-inch (4-cm) cubes (see Variation)

Sauce

4 tbsp (60 ml) neutral oil of choice, divided

½ tsp cumin seeds

¼ tsp asafetida

1 large onion, minced

Salt, as needed

½-inch (1.3-cm) piece fresh ginger, finely grated

2 cloves garlic, finely grated

Start by making the marinade. In a large bowl, whisk together the Greek yogurt, garlic, ginger, Kashmiri red chili powder, red chili powder, Easy Garam Masala, mustard oil and salt. Add the chicken and toss it in the marinade, ensuring all of the pieces are evenly coated. Marinate the chicken on the counter while you prep the rest of the ingredients. Alternatively, if you have time, marinate the chicken in the refrigerator for up to 8 hours or overnight. If you marinate the chicken in the refrigerator, let the chicken sit out on the counter for 30 to 60 minutes before cooking it.

To make the sauce, place the inner pot in the Instant Pot and press the **Sauté** button. When the display shows "Hot," add 2 tablespoons (30 ml) of the oil, the cumin seeds and asafetida. When the seeds sizzle and the asafetida froths, add the onion. Sprinkle the mixture with some salt to help the onion soften. Sauté the onion for 8 to 10 minutes, stirring it frequently, until it is golden brown.

Stir in the ginger and garlic and sauté the mixture for 1 minute. Add the turmeric, ground cumin, coriander, Easy Garam Masala and Kashmiri red chili powder. Sauté the mixture for 30 seconds to let the spices bloom.

Mix in the tomatoes and stir to combine the ingredients. Deglaze the bottom of the pot by scraping it with a wooden spoon. This is an important step; if the bottom of the pot is not deglazed well, the "burn" error might appear during the pressure-cooking stage.

Cook the mixture for 5 minutes, until the tomatoes lose most of their moisture. Press the **Cancel** button to turn off the Instant Pot. Add the water and stir to combine it with the other ingredients. Deglaze the bottom of the pot again if needed. Also, taste the mixture and adjust the seasonings if needed.

(continued)

Chicken Tikka Masala *(continued)*

½ tsp ground turmeric

½ tsp ground cumin

½ tsp ground coriander

1 tsp Easy Garam Masala (page 172)

1 tbsp (6 g) Kashmiri red chili powder

3 medium tomatoes, pureed

¼ cup (60 ml) water

¼ cup (60 ml) heavy cream

2 tsp (1 g) kasuri methi (dried fenugreek leaves), crushed

4 to 5 sprigs fresh cilantro, leaves roughly chopped, for garnishing

For Serving

Tandoori naan, rotis or laccha parathas

Steamed basmati rice

Variation

• Turn this recipe into a vegetarian paneer tikka masala by substituting the chicken with cubed paneer cheese. Marinate the paneer cubes in the same marinade as you would the chicken, but do not cook them in the steamer basket along with the sauce. Instead, broil the cheese like you would the cooked chicken in the recipe. Finally, decrease the cooking time for the sauce to 5 minutes, then combine the broiled paneer with the cooked sauce.

To cook the chicken and the sauce, place a tall trivet in the inner pot, over the tomato-onion sauce (see Notes).

Transfer the marinated chicken pieces to a steamer basket and place it over the trivet. Close the Instant Pot's lid and turn the steam-release valve to the sealing position. Press the **Poultry** or **Manual/Pressure Cook** button and set the timer for 10 minutes at **high pressure**. When the cooking is complete, allow the pressure to release naturally—which will take 15 to 20 minutes—and then open the lid.

While the Instant Pot depressurizes, preheat the broiler. Line a medium nonstick baking sheet with aluminum foil and lightly grease the foil with about ½ tablespoon (8 ml) of oil. Using a pair of tongs, transfer the cooked chicken pieces to the prepared baking sheet. Gently separate them with the tongs so that they are not touching.

Brush the chicken pieces with the remaining 1½ tablespoons (22 ml) of oil. Broil the chicken for 2 to 3 minutes, until they are lightly charred. Take the baking sheet out of the oven, flip the chicken pieces and broil them for 2 to 3 minutes on the other side.

To bring the dish together, remove the trivet from the inner pot and press the **Sauté** button to help the sauce thicken. Cook the sauce, stirring it frequently, for about 2 minutes. Add the broiled chicken pieces. Toss the chicken gently to combine them with the sauce.

Press the **Cancel** button to turn off the Instant Pot. Press the **Keep Warm** button. Pour in the heavy cream, then add the kasuri methi and stir the mixture gently, but do not overmix the ingredients. Close the lid and let the flavors blend and develop for 10 to 15 minutes, or until you are ready to serve.

Garnish the dish with the cilantro. Serve it with warm naan or steamed basmati rice.

Notes:

• Kashmiri red chili powder gives the chicken and the sauce their vibrant red color. You can substitute mild Hungarian paprika or tandoori masala, which is available in Indian stores or on Amazon.

• If you don't have a steamer basket, broil the chicken first per the directions in the recipe, adding an additional ¼ cup (60 ml) of water to avoid the "burn" error, and then add it to the sauce. Follow the remaining steps in the recipe.

Ball Curry

(Meatball Curry)

This traditional recipe for making tender, juicy meatballs cooked in a spicy curry comes from my husband's family, who is from Chennai, in the southern part of India. This is his grandmother's recipe, which was passed down to me by my mother-in-law, and I learned it in the first week that I spent with them right after my husband and I married.

I retrofitted the recipe to accommodate the Instant Pot, as I think making meatballs in the Instant Pot is the easiest and best method—they don't fall apart or dry out like they do when they are pan-fried or baked in the oven. Simply drop them in the curry and cook everything together. The curry gets infused with meaty flavor and tastes amazing!

Serves 4

Meatballs
1½ lb (681 g) ground chicken thigh meat (see Variations)

2 tsp (4 g) Easy Garam Masala (page 172)

½ tsp ground turmeric

Salt, as needed

Red pepper flakes, as needed

4 to 5 sprigs fresh cilantro, tender parts of stems and leaves minced

1 medium green onion, minced

Paste
1 large onion, peeled and quartered

⅓ cup (33 g) grated fresh or thawed frozen coconut

2 to 3 green bird's eye chilies, halved (see Variations)

4 cloves garlic, smashed and peeled

1-inch (2.5-cm) piece fresh ginger, roughly chopped

Start by preparing the meatball mixture. In a medium bowl, combine the chicken, Easy Garam Masala, turmeric, salt, red pepper flakes, cilantro and green onion. Mix until the ingredients are just combined. Do not mash the meat or overwork the mixture. Set the meatball mixture aside.

Prepare the paste. In a blender or food processor, combine the onion, coconut, bird's-eye chilies, garlic and ginger. Blend the ingredients until they form a smooth paste. Set the paste aside.

Variations
- You can switch it up and make the recipe with any type of ground meat—try turkey, lamb, beef or pork.
- If you prefer a milder curry, use serrano or jalapeño chilies for less heat.
- Make it vegetarian by using baby potatoes instead of meatballs and use water or vegetable stock in place of chicken stock.

(continued)

Ball Curry *(continued)*

Curry

2 tbsp (30 g) coconut oil or neutral oil of choice, plus more as needed

½ tsp cumin seeds

½ tsp mustard seeds

¼ tsp asafetida

Salt, as needed

½ tsp ground turmeric

½ tsp ground cumin

½ tsp ground coriander

1 tsp Easy Garam Masala (page 172)

2 medium tomatoes, pureed

2 cups (480 ml) chicken stock or water

4 to 5 sprigs fresh cilantro, leaves roughly chopped, for garnishing

For Serving

Steamed Ponni rice or basmati rice (see Notes)

Plain, unsweetened Greek yogurt (optional)

Vadu mango pickle (see Notes; optional)

To make the curry, place the inner pot in the Instant Pot and press the **Sauté** button. When the display reads "Hot," add the coconut oil and allow it to melt. Add the cumin seeds, mustard seeds and asafetida. When the seeds sizzle and the asafetida froths, add the paste. Season the mixture with salt and sauté it for 8 to 10 minutes, stirring frequently to ensure it cooks evenly, until the paste loses most of its moisture and leaves the sides of the pot, coming together in a cohesive mass. It should not have a raw smell and should be a light brown color. Don't worry if the bottom of the pot looks burnt; it will be deglazed with the addition of the tomatoes and stock later.

Add the turmeric, ground cumin, coriander and Easy Garam Masala. Cook the mixture for about 30 seconds, stirring it vigorously and constantly, and then mix in the tomatoes. Deglaze the bottom of the pot by scraping it with a wooden spoon and mix everything well. This is an important step; if the pot is not deglazed well, the "burn" error might appear during the pressure-cooking stage.

Season the mixture with salt and stir it well. Cook for 5 minutes, until the tomatoes lose most of their moisture and the whole mixture turns into a thick paste. Press the **Cancel** button to turn off the Instant Pot. Pour in the chicken stock and stir to combine the ingredients. Deglaze the bottom of the pot again if needed. Also, taste the mixture and adjust the seasonings if needed.

Rub a little additional coconut oil on your palms. Shape the meatball mixture into approximately 1-inch (2.5-cm) round meatballs between your palms and gently drop them into the pot with the curry, making sure not to stack the meatballs on top of one another. Alternatively, use a mini ice cream scoop to shape the meatballs and directly drop them into the pot.

Once all the meatballs are in the curry, do not touch or move them. Close the lid and turn the steam-release valve to the sealing position. Press the **Poultry** or **Manual/Pressure Cook** button and set the timer for 10 minutes at **high pressure**. When the cooking is complete, allow the pressure to release naturally—which will take 15 to 20 minutes—and then open the lid.

Garnish the curry with the cilantro. Serve it spooned over a bed of steamed rice along with some Greek yogurt (if using) and Vadu mango pickle (if using).

Notes:

• Ponni rice is grown in Tamil Nadu state.

• Vadu mango pickle is a traditional South Indian pickle made with baby mangoes, mustard seeds and red chilies. It's a classic pairing with this dish but is also great with many other South Indian dishes in the book. It can be easily found in Indian grocery stores or online.

Pudina Gosht

(Minty Lamb Curry)

Lamb and mint are a match made in heaven, and the classic pairing was the inspiration behind this not-too-spicy lamb curry! To double down on the minty flavor for the curry, I marinate the lamb with lots of fresh mint mixed with some spiced yogurt. I also use a fresh paste of cilantro, green chilies and, of course, mint, to make the curry.

I've made this curry on the stove, but the stovetop version doesn't compare to how flavorful this dish becomes when it's cooked in the Instant Pot. The mint and spices get locked into the meat under pressure, resulting in a simply delicious curry with melt-in-your-mouth lamb.

Serves 3 to 4

Marinade

⅓ cup (80 ml) plain, unsweetened Greek yogurt

1 cup (32 g) tightly packed fresh mint leaves

1 tbsp (6 g) meat masala (see Note)

Salt, as needed

½ tsp freshly ground black pepper

1½ lb (681 g) boneless lamb stew meat, cut into 1½-inch (4-cm) cubes and trimmed of visible fat (see Variations)

Paste

¼ cup (8 g) tightly packed fresh mint leaves

¼ cup (4 g) tightly packed fresh cilantro leaves

1 to 2 green bird's-eye chilies, roughly chopped or broken into pieces (see Variations)

Start by preparing the marinade. In a large bowl, whisk together the Greek yogurt, mint leaves, meat masala, salt and black pepper. Add the lamb and toss it in the marinade, ensuring all of the pieces are evenly coated. Allow the lamb to marinate on the counter while you prepare the rest of the recipe. Alternatively, if you have time, marinate the lamb in the refrigerator for up to 8 hours or overnight. If you marinate the lamb in the refrigerator, let the meat sit out on the counter for 30 to 60 minutes before cooking it.

To make the paste, combine the mint leaves, cilantro leaves and bird's-eye chilies in a blender, mini food processor or spice grinder. Pulse the ingredients a few times to create a coarse paste. Set the paste aside.

Note: Meat masala is readily available in Indian stores or on Amazon. If you cannot find it, though, you can substitute it with the same amount of Easy Garam Masala (page 172) and ½ teaspoon ground mustard or ½ teaspoon Dijon mustard.

Variations

• Substitute lamb with cubes of boneless, skinless chicken thigh meat chunks to make pudina murgh. Decrease the cooking time to 10 minutes.

• If you prefer a milder curry, use serrano or jalapeño peppers for less heat.

• Make it vegetarian by substituting lamb with baby potatoes to make pudina aloo. Prick the potatoes in several places with a fork before tossing them in the marinade. Decrease the cooking time to 5 minutes.

(continued)

Pudina Gosht *(continued)*

Curry

2 tbsp (30 ml) neutral oil of choice

1 tsp cumin seeds

¼ tsp asafetida

1 large onion, minced

Salt, as needed

½-inch (1.3-cm) piece fresh ginger, finely grated

2 cloves garlic, finely grated

½ tsp ground turmeric

½ tsp ground cumin

½ tsp ground coriander

1 tbsp (16 g) tomato paste

2 medium tomatoes, pureed

¼ cup (60 ml) water

Fresh mint leaves, for garnishing

For Serving

Tandoori naan, rotis or laccha parathas

Steamed basmati rice

To make the curry, place the inner pot in the Instant Pot and press the **Sauté** button. When the display reads "Hot," add the oil, cumin seeds and asafetida. When the seeds sizzle and the asafetida froths, add the paste. Let the paste sizzle for 30 seconds, then add the onion. Season the mixture with salt to help the onion soften. Sauté the mixture, stirring it frequently, for 5 to 7 minutes, until the onion is translucent.

Stir in the ginger and garlic and sauté the mixture for 1 minute. Add the turmeric, ground cumin and coriander. Sauté the mixture for 30 seconds to let the spices bloom. Add the tomato paste and the pureed tomatoes and stir to combine the ingredients. Deglaze the bottom of the pot by scraping it with a wooden spoon. This is an important step; if the bottom of the pot is not deglazed well, the "burn" error might appear during the pressure-cooking stage.

Season the curry with additional salt and stir to combine the ingredients well. Cook the curry for 5 minutes, until the tomatoes lose most of their moisture. Press the **Cancel** button to turn off the Instant Pot. Add the water and stir to combine the ingredients. Taste the curry and adjust the seasonings if needed.

Stir in the marinated lamb and ensure that all of the pieces are coated evenly with the sauce. Close the Instant Pot's lid and turn the steam-release valve to the sealing position. Press the **Meat/Stew** button and set the timer for 30 minutes at **high pressure**. When the cooking is complete, allow the pressure to release naturally—which will take 15 to 20 minutes—and then open the lid.

Garnish the curry with the mint leaves and serve it with naan or steamed basmati rice.

Murgh Malaiwala

(Chicken in Herbed Cream Sauce)

Murgh malaiwala is a mildly spiced and luscious cream-based chicken curry that gets its silky smooth texture from the heavy cream and almond paste used in the base sauce. Even though it's a mild curry, it packs a ton of flavor from the herbs and spices that go in both the marinade for the chicken and the base sauce.

In the original recipe, the chicken is marinated overnight before it is grilled and added to the cream sauce. But with the Instant Pot, this recipe is easy to whip up even on a weeknight. Simply toss the chicken in the marinade while you prep the rest of the ingredients and throw it in the pot!

Serves 4

Marinade

¼ cup (60 ml) plain, unsweetened Greek yogurt

2 tbsp (30 ml) heavy cream

2 cloves garlic, finely grated

½-inch (1.3-cm) piece fresh ginger, finely grated

½ tsp Easy Garam Masala (page 172)

½ tsp freshly ground black pepper

Red pepper flakes, as needed

2 tsp (1 g) kasuri methi (dried fenugreek leaves), crushed

9 to 10 sprigs fresh cilantro, leaves finely chopped

Salt, as needed

Juice of ½ medium lemon

1½ lb (681 g) boneless, skinless chicken thighs, cut into 1½-inch (4-cm) pieces (see Variations)

Begin by preparing the marinade. In a large bowl, whisk together the Greek yogurt, cream, garlic, ginger, Easy Garam Masala, black pepper, red pepper flakes, kasuri methi, cilantro, salt and lemon juice. Add the chicken and toss it in the marinade, ensuring all the pieces are evenly coated. Marinate the chicken on the counter while you prepare the rest of the recipe. Alternatively, if you have time, marinate the chicken in the refrigerator for up to 8 hours or overnight. However, if you marinate the chicken in the refrigerator, do not add the lemon juice to the marinade until 30 to 60 minutes before cooking the chicken—let the chicken marinate on the counter during this time.

Variations

• Use boneless lamb in place of chicken to make malai lamb.

• You can replace boneless chicken with bone-in, skinless chicken thighs and drumsticks to make the traditional version. Be sure to increase the cooking time to 15 minutes.

• Make it vegetarian by substituting chicken with baby potatoes to make malaiwale aloo. Prick the potatoes in several places with a fork before tossing them in the marinade. Decrease the cooking time to 5 minutes.

(continued)

Murgh Malaiwala *(continued)*

Curry

2 tbsp (30 ml) neutral oil of choice

1 tsp cumin seeds

¼ tsp asafetida

1 medium onion, minced

Salt, as needed

½ tsp ground cumin

½ tsp ground coriander

1 tsp Easy Garam Masala (page 172)

¼ cup (65 g) raw almond butter or ¼ cup (24 g) almond flour

¾ cup (180 ml) water, divided

¼ cup (60 ml) heavy cream

Fresh cilantro leaves, for garnishing

For Serving

Tandoori naan, rotis or laccha parathas

Steamed basmati rice

Thickly sliced red onion (optional)

Green bird's-eye chilies, serrano chilies or jalapeño chilies (optional)

To make the curry, place the inner pot in the Instant Pot and press the **Sauté** button. When the display reads "Hot," add the oil, cumin seeds and asafetida. When the seeds sizzle and the asafetida froths, add the onion. Season the onion with salt to help it soften. Sauté the onion for 5 to 7 minutes, stirring it frequently, until it is translucent.

Add the ground cumin, coriander and Easy Garam Masala and sauté the mixture for 30 seconds to let the spices bloom.

Press the **Cancel** button to turn off the Instant Pot.

Add the almond butter and ½ cup (120 ml) of the water and stir to combine the ingredients well. Sauté the mixture on the residual heat for 2 to 3 minutes, stirring it constantly while scraping the bottom of the pot with a wooden spoon, if needed, until the almond paste loses most of its moisture. Taste the mixture and adjust the seasonings if needed.

Add the marinated chicken along with the remaining ¼ cup (60 ml) of water. Toss the chicken with the curry mixture and stir to combine the ingredients.

Close the Instant Pot's lid and turn the steam-release valve to the sealing position. Press the **Poultry** or **Manual/Pressure Cook** button and set the timer for 10 minutes at **high pressure**. When the cooking is complete, allow the pressure to release naturally—which will take about 15 minutes—and then open the lid.

Stir in the heavy cream. Garnish with fresh cilantro leaves and serve the curry warm with naan and rice, along with red onion (if using) and green chilies (if using).

Lamb Kala Masala

(Lamb in Onion-Coconut Curry)

Kala masala, the cornerstone spice mix of Maharashtrian cuisine, was the inspiration behind this moderately spicy and smoky lamb curry. In this recipe, I use some of the typical spices that go in the traditional kala masala—like sesame seeds, poppy seeds, black pepper, cinnamon, dried red chilies and dried coconut—and fry them with onions until the mixture turns dark brown in color and looks almost burnt. It is then ground to a thick paste and used as the base for this lamb curry, to be cooked easily in the Instant Pot!

Serves 4 to 6

Marinade

2 lb (908 g) bone-in lamb stew meat, cut into 1½-inch (4-cm) cubes and trimmed of visible fat (see Variations)

Salt, as needed

1 tbsp (6 g) Easy Garam Masala (page 172)

Red chili powder, as needed

½ tsp ground turmeric

½ tsp ground cumin

½ tsp ground coriander

½ tsp finely ground black pepper

½-inch (1.3-cm) piece fresh ginger, finely grated

2 cloves garlic, finely grated

Kala Masala

4 tbsp (60 ml) neutral oil of choice, divided

1 large onion, thinly sliced

Salt, as needed

5 to 6 dried spicy red chilies, stems discarded (see Variations)

1 tsp sesame seeds

2 tsp (6 g) khus khus (white poppy seeds)

1 tbsp (6 g) coriander seeds

3 to 4 whole cloves

1 to 2 dried bay leaves

Begin by preparing the marinade. In a large bowl, combine the lamb, salt, Easy Garam Masala, red chili powder, turmeric, cumin, ground coriander, black pepper, ginger and garlic. Make sure each piece of meat is covered evenly with the marinade. Marinate the lamb on the counter while you prepare the rest of the recipe.

To make the kala masala, place the inner pot in the Instant Pot and press the **Sauté** button. When the display reads "Hot," add 2 tablespoons (30 ml) of the oil and the onion. Season the onion with salt to help it soften. Sauté the onion for 8 to 10 minutes, stirring it frequently, until it is golden brown.

Add the red chilies, sesame seeds, khus khus, coriander seeds, cloves, bay leaves, black peppercorns, cinnamon bark and coconut. Sauté the mixture for 5 to 7 minutes, until the coconut is golden brown and the spices are fragrant.

Press the **Cancel** button to turn off the Instant Pot. Pour in ½ cup (120 ml) of the water and deglaze the bottom of the pot by scraping it with a wooden spoon. Let the onion-coconut mixture cool for 5 to 10 minutes.

When the mixture has cooled off a bit, transfer it to a high-powered food grinder or blender and grind it to a smooth paste. Add a little additional water if needed. Taste the paste and adjust the seasonings if needed. Set the paste aside.

Wipe out the inner pot with a paper towel and place the clean pot back in the Instant Pot. Press the **Sauté** button. When the display reads "Hot," add the remaining 2 tablespoons (30 ml) of oil. Add the marinated lamb and spread it across the bottom of the inner pot in an even layer. Sear the lamb, without touching it, for about 2 minutes. Flip the pieces of meat and let them sear on the other side for 2 minutes.

Press the **Cancel** button. Add the remaining 1 cup (240 ml) of water and deglaze the bottom of the pot by scraping it with a wooden spoon.

(continued)

Lamb Kala Masala *(continued)*

6 to 8 black peppercorns

1-inch (2.5-cm) piece cinnamon bark

¼ cup (30 g) unsweetened coconut flakes or ¼ cup (23 g) unsweetened shredded or desiccated coconut

1½ cups (360 ml) water, plus more as needed, divided

4 to 5 sprigs fresh cilantro, leaves roughly chopped, for garnishing

For Serving

Steamed Ambemohar rice or basmati rice (see Note)

Jowar bhakri (unleavened sorghum-flour bread; optional)

Rustic Kanda Lasun Masala (page 176; optional)

Thickly sliced red onion (optional)

Green bird's-eye chilies, serrano chilies or jalapeño chilies (optional)

Transfer the ground kala masala paste to the pot and toss the ingredients well to combine them, making sure all the pieces of meat are coated well. Close the Instant Pot's lid and turn the steam-release valve to the sealing position. Press the **Meat/Stew** button and set the timer for 40 minutes at **high pressure**. When the cooking is complete, allow the pressure to release naturally—which will take 15 to 20 minutes—and then open the lid.

Garnish the curry with the cilantro. Serve it warm with the Ambemohar rice, jowar bhakri (if using), Rustic Kanda Lasun Masala (if using), red onion (if using) and green chilies (if using).

Note: Ambemohar rice is a variety grown in Maharashtra state.

Variations

• Substitute lamb with bone-in, skinless chicken drumsticks and thighs and decrease the cooking time to 15 minutes.

• For a milder flavor, deseed the chilies or use milder ones, like dried Kashmiri red chilies.

Methi Murgh Handi
(Fenugreek Chicken Curry)

Murgh or chicken handi is a moderately spicy, rustic curry that is cooked in a clay pot, or a handi. While handis are a rare sight in today's home kitchens, Instant Pots are not! This version of chicken handi is inspired by my sister, who adds fresh fenugreek leaves to her chicken curry recipe. I love the hint of mildly bitter flavor that fenugreek adds to the overall dish, taking a humble chicken handi to a whole new level!

Serves 4

Marinade

½ cup (120 ml) plain, unsweetened Greek yogurt

2 cloves garlic, finely grated

½-inch (1.3-cm) piece fresh ginger, finely grated

Red chili powder, to taste

1 tsp Easy Garam Masala (page 172)

½ tsp ground turmeric

Salt, as needed

2 lb (908 g) bone-in, skinless chicken drumsticks and thighs (see Variations)

Curry

2 tbsp (30 ml) melted ghee or neutral oil of choice

1 tsp cumin seeds

¼ tsp asafetida

1 large onion, thinly sliced

Salt, as needed

½-inch (1.3-cm) piece fresh ginger, finely grated

2 cloves garlic, finely grated

½ tsp ground turmeric

½ tsp ground cumin

½ tsp ground coriander

1 tsp Easy Garam Masala (page 172)

1 medium tomato, diced

⅓ cup (80 ml) water

Start by preparing the marinade. In a large bowl, whisk together the Greek yogurt, garlic, ginger, red chili powder, Easy Garam Masala, turmeric and salt. Add the chicken and toss it in the marinade, ensuring all the pieces are evenly coated. Marinate the chicken on the counter while you prepare the rest of the recipe. Alternatively, if you have time, marinate the chicken in the refrigerator for up to 8 hours or overnight. If you marinate the chicken in the refrigerator, let the chicken sit out on the counter for 30 to 60 minutes before cooking it.

To make the curry, place the inner pot in the Instant Pot and press the **Sauté** button. When the display reads "Hot," add the ghee, cumin seeds and asafetida. When the seeds sizzle and the asafetida froths, add the onion. Season the onion with salt to help it soften. Sauté the onion for 5 to 7 minutes, stirring it frequently, until it becomes translucent.

Stir in the ginger and garlic and sauté the mixture for 1 minute. Add the turmeric, ground cumin, coriander and Easy Garam Masala. Sauté the mixture for 30 seconds to let the spices bloom.

Add the tomato, season the mixture with salt and stir to combine the ingredients. Cook the mixture for 5 minutes, stirring it frequently, until the tomato loses most of its moisture.

Press the **Cancel** button to turn off the Instant Pot.

Add the water and deglaze the bottom of the pot by scraping it with a wooden spoon. This is an important step; if the bottom of the pot is not deglazed well, the "burn" error might appear during the pressure-cooking stage.

(continued)

Methi Murgh Handi *(continued)*

2 cups (66 g) fresh fenugreek leaves, roughly chopped (see Variations)

For Serving

Tandoori naan, rotis or laccha parathas (optional)

Steamed basmati rice (optional)

Red pearl onions, peeled and trimmed (optional)

Green bird's-eye chilies, serrano chilies or jalapeño chilies (optional)

Taste the mixture and adjust the seasonings if needed. Stir in the fenugreek leaves and marinated chicken, ensuring everything is combined well.

Close the Instant Pot's lid and turn the steam-release valve to the sealing position. Press the **Poultry** or **Manual/Pressure Cook** button and set the timer for 15 minutes at **high pressure**. When the cooking is complete, allow the pressure to release naturally—which will take 15 to 20 minutes—and then open the lid.

Serve the curry warm with the naan (if using) or basmati rice (if using), with the red pearl onions (if using) and green chilies (if using) on the side.

Variations

- You can use boneless chicken thighs in this recipe. Decrease the cooking time to 10 minutes.

- Make it vegetarian by substituting the chicken with baby potatoes. Prick the potatoes in several places with a fork before tossing them in the marinade. Decrease the cooking time to 5 minutes.

- Swap fenugreek for spinach or mustard greens.

Laal Maas

(Lamb in Red Curry)

Laal maas is a flavorful curry from the western state of Rajasthan. The name literally translates to "red meat" because of the red curry in which chunks of lamb or goat are cooked, although you can find variations with chicken as well. The curry is not as spicy as it looks. The traditional dish gets its vibrant red color from the dried Mathania red chilies that are native to the area. The chilies are difficult to find and can be substituted with the more easily available Kashmiri red chilies, which is what I use. With its mildly delicious flavor that comes from the spices, this lamb stew is a weeknight win for the entire family!

Serves 4

Marinade

⅓ cup (80 ml) plain, unsweetened Greek yogurt

Salt, as needed

½ tsp ground turmeric

1 tbsp (6 g) Kashmiri red chili powder (see Notes)

Red chili powder, as needed

2 cloves garlic, finely grated

½-inch (1.3-cm) piece fresh ginger, finely grated

2 lb (908 g) bone-in lamb stew meat, cut into 1½-inch (4-cm) cubes and trimmed of visible fat (see Variations)

Curry

2 tbsp (30 ml) mustard oil or neutral oil of choice

½ tsp cumin seeds

2 dried bay leaves

2 to 3 (1-inch [2.5-cm]) pieces cinnamon bark

5 to 6 black peppercorns

1 pod black cardamom

5 whole cloves

1 large onion, thinly sliced

Salt, as needed

5 to 6 cloves garlic, peeled

1 cup (240 ml) water

Begin by preparing the marinade. In a large bowl, whisk together the Greek yogurt, salt, turmeric, Kashmiri red chili powder, red chili powder, garlic and ginger. Add the lamb and toss it in the marinade, ensuring all the pieces are evenly coated. Marinate the lamb on the counter while you prepare the rest of the recipe. Alternatively, if you have time, marinate the lamb in the refrigerator for up to 8 hours or overnight. If you marinate the lamb in the refrigerator, let the meat sit out on the counter for 30 to 60 minutes before cooking it.

To make the curry, place the inner pot in the Instant Pot and press the **Sauté** button. When the display reads "Hot," add the mustard oil, cumin seeds, bay leaves, cinnamon bark pieces, peppercorns, cardamom and cloves. Let the spices sizzle in the hot oil for 30 to 60 seconds, and then stir in the onion. Season the onion with salt to help it soften. Sauté the onion-spice mixture for about 5 minutes, until the onion is translucent.

Add the garlic cloves and sauté the mixture for about 5 minutes, stirring it frequently, until the garlic is soft and the onion is golden brown.

Press the **Cancel** button to turn off the Instant Pot. Add the marinated lamb and stir the ingredients to combine them well. Pour in the water and stir to combine everything.

(continued)

Beef Ularthiyathu *(continued)*

Sauce

2 tbsp (30 ml) melted coconut oil
or neutral oil of choice

1 tsp mustard seeds

¼ tsp asafetida

2 to 3 dried red chilies, stems
removed and deseeded (optional)

5 to 6 fresh curry leaves

8 to 10 Asian shallots, thinly sliced
(see Notes)

Salt, as needed

4 to 5 cloves garlic, peeled and
gently smashed

½ tsp ground turmeric

½ tsp Easy Garam Masala (page 172)

1 small tomato, thinly sliced

¼ cup (60 ml) water

½ cup (120 ml) light coconut milk

Fresh curry leaves, for garnishing

For Serving

Malabar parottas (see Notes)

Thickly sliced red onion (optional)

To make the sauce, place the inner pot in the Instant Pot and press the **Sauté** button. When the display reads "Hot," add the coconut oil, mustard seeds, asafetida, red chilies and curry leaves. When the curry leaves splutter, add the shallots. Season the mixture with salt to help the shallots soften. Sauté the mixture for about 5 minutes, stirring it frequently, until the shallots are translucent.

Add the garlic and sauté the mixture for 2 to 3 minutes, until the shallots are light brown and the garlic has softened.

Add the turmeric and Easy Garam Masala. Sauté the mixture for about 1 minute to let the spices bloom. Add the tomato, season the mixture with salt and sauté the ingredients for about 1 minute, until the tomato has softened.

Pour in the water and deglaze the bottom of the pot by scraping it with a wooden spoon. This is an important step; if the bottom of the pot is not deglazed well, the "burn" error might appear during the pressure-cooking stage.

Press the **Cancel** button to turn off the Instant Pot. Continue to sauté the onion-tomato mixture and let its moisture evaporate from the pot's residual heat. Taste the mixture and adjust the seasonings if needed.

Add the marinated beef and stir the ingredients to combine them well. Pour in the coconut milk and stir to combine the ingredients. Close the Instant Pot's lid and turn the steam-release valve to the sealing position. Press the **Meat/Stew** button and set the timer for 10 minutes at **high pressure**. When the cooking is complete, open the lid using a quick pressure release to depressurize the Instant Pot. Press the **Cancel** button to turn off the Instant Pot.

Using a slotted spoon, transfer the cooked beef to a clean medium bowl.

Press the **Sauté** button and bring the sauce to a boil. Stir the sauce continuously for 5 to 7 minutes, until most of the moisture is evaporated and the oil has separated from the sauce.

Transfer the beef back to the reduced sauce and toss to combine it well with the sauce. Press the **Cancel** button to turn off the Instant Pot.

Garnish the beef roast with the curry leaves. Serve it warm with the Malabar parottas and red onion (if using).

Pandhra Rassa

(Chicken in Mild Coconut Curry)

While Kolhapur, a city in the southern part of Maharashtra state, is famous for its very spicy cuisine, it is also the home of this relatively mild coconut curry, which is made with either chicken or lamb.

This flavorful curry uses three forms of coconut—dried coconut, fresh coconut and coconut milk—and gets its characteristic warmth from the use of black pepper and a hint of heat from green chilies. The traditional recipe is a long, two-step process in which the meat is cooked separately in a spiced broth and then combined with the coconut curry that is simmering on the side. The Instant Pot cuts the process down to a single cooking step and gets it done in half the time.

Serves 4

Pandhra Masala

1 tbsp (9 g) khus khus (white poppy seeds)

1 tsp white sesame seeds

¼ cup (60 ml) hot water

½ tsp black peppercorns

3 to 4 green bird's-eye chilies, roughly chopped (see Variations)

¼ cup (30 g) unsweetened coconut flakes or ¼ cup (23 g) unsweetened shredded or desiccated coconut

¾ cup (75 g) fresh or thawed frozen grated coconut

¼ cup (24 g) blanched almond flour (preferably superfine)

1 cup (240 ml) coconut milk

Curry

2 tbsp (30 ml) melted coconut oil or neutral oil of choice

½ tsp cumin seeds

¼ tsp asafetida

3 to 4 black peppercorns

4 to 5 whole cloves

1 to 2 dried bay leaves

1-inch (2.5-cm) piece cinnamon bark

Begin by preparing the pandhra masala. In a small bowl, soak the poppy seeds and sesame seeds in the hot water for about 15 minutes.

Transfer the poppy seeds, sesame seeds and soaking water to a high-powered food grinder or blender. Add the peppercorns, bird's-eye chilies, flaked coconut, grated coconut, almond flour and coconut milk. Process the ingredients to a fine, smooth paste. Set the paste aside.

To make the curry, place the inner pot in the Instant Pot and press the **Sauté** button. When the display reads "Hot," add the oil, cumin seeds, asafetida, peppercorns, cloves, bay leaves and cinnamon bark. Let the spices sizzle in the hot oil for 30 to 60 seconds, and then stir in the onion. Season the mixture with salt to help the onion soften. Sauté the mixture for about 5 minutes, until the onion is translucent.

Stir in the garlic and ginger. Sauté the mixture for 3 to 4 minutes, until it is light brown. Add the Easy Garam Masala and sauté the mixture for 30 seconds to let the spices in the Easy Garam Masala bloom.

Add the pandhra masala, season the mixture with additional salt and stir the ingredients well to combine them. Sauté the ingredients for 5 to 7 minutes, until the mixture thickens and turns a light brown color.

Pour in the water and deglaze the bottom of the pot by scraping it with a wooden spoon. This is an important step; if the bottom of the pot is not deglazed well, the "burn" error might appear during the pressure-cooking stage.

Press the **Cancel** button to turn off the Instant Pot. Taste the curry and adjust the seasonings if needed.

1 large onion, minced

Salt, as needed

2 cloves garlic, finely grated

½-inch (1.3-cm) piece fresh ginger, finely grated

1 tsp Easy Garam Masala (page 172)

½ cup (120 ml) water

2 lb (908 g) bone-in, skinless chicken drumsticks and thighs (see Variations)

4 to 5 sprigs fresh cilantro, leaves roughly chopped (optional), for garnishing

For Serving

Steamed Ambemohar rice or basmati rice

Chapati (unleavened whole wheat bread; optional) or jowar bhakri (unleavened sorghum-flour bread; optional)

Rustic Kanda Lasun Masala (page 176; optional)

Add the chicken and stir the ingredients to combine everything well. Close the Instant Pot's lid and turn the steam-release valve to the sealing position. Press the **Poultry** or **Manual/Pressure Cook** button and set the timer for 15 minutes at **high pressure**. When the cooking is complete, allow the pressure to release naturally—which will take 15 to 20 minutes—and then open the lid.

Garnish the curry with the cilantro (if using). Serve the curry warm with the steamed rice, chapati or jowar bhakri (if using) and Rustic Kanda Lasun Masala (if using).

Variations

- If you prefer a milder curry, use jalapeño peppers instead of the bird's-eye chilies.

- You can substitute boneless chicken thighs for bone-in pieces. Decrease the cooking time to 10 minutes.

- You can use bone-in lamb or goat meat in this recipe. Increase the cooking time to 40 minutes.

- Make this dish vegan by substituting the chicken with 1 (15-ounce [425-g]) can of chickpeas. Drain and rinse the chickpeas prior to adding them to the dish. Use the same settings for time and pressure as directed in the recipe.

Wholesome Bowls

As a full-time working mom, I'm a huge fan of wholesome bowls that I can put together and either bring to work, pack for the family for their lunches or serve for dinners after busy, long days. They're hearty, healthy, one-pot meals and come together fairly quickly. Thank you, Instant Pot!

The bowls in this chapter range from lighter fare, like Saar (Spicy Tomato Soup; page 56), to heartier meals like the Szechuan Noodles (Spaghetti in Szechuan Sauce; page 45). There are quite a few soups included in this chapter: Palakachi Patal Bhaji (Spinach and Buttermilk Soup; page 52), which is a traditional Maharashtrian recipe with buttermilk and spinach; an Indian-Chinese restaurant favorite, Manchow Soup (Chicken and Vegetable Soup; page 55); and one of my fusion creations, Chana Masala Soup (Spicy Chickpea Soup; page 51), which looks and feels just like Tuscan bean soup but has the classic flavors of the popular Indian chickpea curry chana masala.

Being a huge fan of spaghetti squash, I'm sharing how I use it to put a healthy twist on a classic starchy potato recipe, Kees (Spiced Spaghetti Squash Hash; page 42), to turn it into a low-carb dish that not only looks good but also tastes much better than the original. If you love spicy food, you're going to be happy with the Misal (Sprouted Beans Stew; page 47), which is one of the spiciest foods from my home state of Maharashtra and popular all over India. It's zesty, hearty and pretty healthy, given that it's made with sprouted beans. Lastly, Rajma Chawal (Red Kidney Beans and Wild Rice; page 59) and Anda Curry (Poached Eggs in Curry; page 40) are there to offer you comforting hugs in a bowl whenever you need them!

Anda Curry

(Poached Eggs in Curry)

Anda curry is a classic Indian dish, and while there are a couple of different versions, the eggs are usually hard-boiled and then added to the curry. However, my husband makes his by cracking the eggs directly into the pot of curry. Doing so is a time-saver, and the eggs are more flavorful when they're poached in the curried broth. We also like to add okra for some contrasting color and a delicious crunch.

Serves 3 to 4

2 tbsp (30 ml) neutral oil of choice

½ tsp cumin seeds

¼ tsp asafetida

1 large onion, minced

Salt, as needed

½-inch (1.3-cm) piece fresh ginger, finely grated

2 cloves garlic, finely grated

½ tsp turmeric

½ tsp ground cumin

½ tsp ground coriander

1 tsp egg curry masala (see Note)

1 tbsp (16 g) tomato paste

3 medium tomatoes, pureed

12 to 15 pods okra, ends trimmed and cut in 3-inch (8-cm)-long sticks (optional)

1 cup (240 ml) water

6 large eggs

4 to 5 sprigs fresh cilantro, leaves roughly chopped, for garnishing

1 medium green onion, thinly sliced, for garnishing

Steamed brown or white basmati rice, for serving

To make the curry, place the inner pot in the Instant Pot and press the **Sauté** button. When the display reads "Hot," add the oil, cumin seeds and asafetida. When the cumin seeds sizzle and the asafetida froths, add the onion. Season the onion with salt to help it soften. Sauté the onion for 5 to 7 minutes, stirring it frequently, until it is translucent.

Stir in the ginger and garlic and sauté the ingredients for 1 minute. Stir in the turmeric, ground cumin, coriander and egg curry masala. Sauté the mixture for about 30 seconds to let the spices bloom, and then add the tomato paste and the pureed tomatoes.

Season the mixture with additional salt and stir the ingredients to combine them well. Deglaze the bottom of the pot by scraping it with a wooden spoon. This is an important step; if the bottom of the pot is not deglazed well, the "burn" error might appear during the pressure-cooking stage.

Cook the mixture for 7 to 8 minutes, until the tomatoes lose almost all of their moisture. Press the **Cancel** button to turn off the Instant Pot. Add the okra (if using). Pour in the water, stirring gently to combine everything. Taste the mixture and adjust the seasonings if needed.

Crack the eggs, one at a time, and gently drop them directly into the curry in separate spots. To make it easier, you can crack the eggs, one at a time, into a small bowl and gently slide each egg into the curry. Once all the eggs are in the curry, do not touch or move them in the pot.

Close the Instant Pot's lid and turn the steam-release valve to the sealing position. Press the **Manual/Pressure Cook** button and set the timer for 1 minute at **high pressure**. For soft-boiled eggs, when the cooking is complete, open the lid using a quick pressure release to depressurize the Instant Pot. For hard-boiled eggs, allow the pressure to release naturally—which will take 11 to 13 minutes—and then open the lid.

Garnish the curry with the cilantro and green onion. Serve the curry over a bed of steamed brown or white basmati rice.

Note: Egg curry masala is available in Indian stores or on Amazon, but you can substitute it with the same amount of Easy Garam Masala (page 172) and ½ teaspoon red chili powder.

Kees

(Spiced Spaghetti Squash Hash)

This is a healthy spin on the classic batatyacha kees (Indian-style spiced shredded-potato hash) that is primarily made on religious fasting days for breakfast or as a side dish. Shredded potatoes tossed with cumin, green chilies and crushed roasted peanuts are pan-fried in ghee and cooked until they are light golden brown. Finished with a good squeeze of lime juice, lots of grated fresh coconut and cilantro, this fasting food is one of my favorites!

After discovering spaghetti squash, I realized its texture is very similar to the shredded-potato hash and swapped it for the potatoes in the original kees recipe. Also, the Instant Pot is more efficient than the oven at cooking the squash!

Serves 2

1 small spaghetti squash

1 cup (240 ml) water

3 tbsp (42 g) ghee or 3 tbsp (45 ml) neutral oil of choice

1 tsp cumin seeds

Red pepper flakes, as needed

Salt, as needed

½ cup (60 g) crushed unsalted roasted peanuts

½ medium lime or lemon

¼ cup (25 g) grated fresh or thawed frozen coconut, divided

18 to 20 sprigs fresh cilantro, leaves roughly chopped, divided

Using a sharp knife, cut the spaghetti squash in half lengthwise; be careful while cutting the squash, as it can be hard and slippery. Then, using a sharp-edged spoon or a fork, carefully scrape out the seeds and stringy flesh. Alternatively, you can cook the squash first and then cut it easily after it has softened. To cook it whole, pierce the squash with a sharp, short knife in 8 to 10 spots all over and then cook it according to the directions in the following paragraphs. When the cooked squash is cool to handle, you can cut it in half lengthwise and scrape the seeds and separate the strands.

Place the inner pot in the Instant Pot and add the water. Place the trivet in the inner pot and place both of the cleaned squash halves on top of it.

Close the Instant Pot's lid and turn the steam-release valve to the sealing position. Press the **Manual/Pressure Cook** button and set the timer for 5 minutes at **high pressure**. This will produce an al dente texture, and the squash will have a slightly crispy bite to it. You can increase the cooking time to 7 or 8 minutes at high pressure for a softer texture.

When the cooking is complete, allow the pressure to release naturally—which will take 12 to 15 minutes—and then open the lid. Press the **Cancel** button to turn off the Instant Pot.

Using oven mitts or a pair of tongs, take the cooked squash halves out of the inner pot. Let them cool until they are easy to handle. In the meantime, drain all the water from the inner pot and dry it with a kitchen towel or paper towel.

When the squash is cool enough to handle, use a fork to carefully scrape and separate the strands of the squash and transfer them to a medium bowl. If desired, you can save the shells to use as serving vessels.

Place the inner pot in the Instant Pot and press the **Sauté** button. When the display reads "Hot," add the ghee and allow it to melt. Add the cumin seeds and red pepper flakes. Let them sizzle for about 30 seconds and then add the squash.

Season the mixture with salt and stir it well, making sure all the squash strands are evenly coated with the ghee, cumin seeds and red pepper flakes. Add the peanuts and stir the ingredients to combine them well.

Press the **Cancel** button. Squeeze the juice of the lime over the squash mixture. Stir in the coconut and cilantro, reserving 1 tablespoon (6 g) of the coconut and 1 tablespoon (1 g) of the cilantro for garnishing. Transfer the kees to the reserved squash shells (if using). Garnish the kees with the reserved coconut and cilantro and serve it immediately.

Chana Masala Soup

(Spicy Chickpea Soup)

This North Indian classic is a regular in my house, but only when my husband is traveling for work! While our daughter and I can happily devour the delicious curry any time, he just doesn't care for it. This fusion recipe has all the flavors of the authentic chickpea stew and comes in the form of a hearty soup. Thankfully, it manages to please my husband's taste buds and satisfies our daughter's and my cravings for chana masala!

Remember to soak the beans for 6 to 8 hours—or overnight—before making this recipe. To save time, you can use canned beans and reduce the pressure-cooking time by half.

Serves 4

½ cup (100 g) dried chickpeas

1½ cups (360 ml) water

2 tbsp (30 ml) neutral oil of choice

½ tsp cumin seeds

1 medium onion, roughly chopped

2 medium carrots, diced

½-inch (1.3-cm) piece fresh ginger, finely grated

2 cloves garlic, finely grated

½ tsp ground cumin

½ tsp ground coriander

1 tbsp (6 g) chhole masala (see Note)

1 tbsp (16 g) tomato paste

3 medium tomatoes, diced

Salt, as needed

4 cups (960 ml) water, vegetable stock or chicken stock

4 leaves kale, stems trimmed and roughly chopped

3 small Yukon gold potatoes, diced

Fresh cilantro leaves, for garnishing

Plain, unsweetened Greek yogurt, for serving (optional)

1 small red onion, thickly sliced, for serving

Lime or lemon wedges, for serving

Naan, for serving (optional)

Soak the chickpeas in 1½ cups (360 ml) water for 8 hours, or up to overnight.

Place the inner pot in the Instant Pot and press the **Sauté** button. When the display reads "Hot," add the oil and cumin seeds. When the seeds sizzle, add in the onion and carrots. Sauté the mixture, stirring it frequently, for 5 to 7 minutes, until the onion is translucent and the carrots have softened a bit.

Stir in the ginger and garlic and sauté for 1 minute. Stir in the ground cumin, coriander and chhole masala. Sauté for about 30 seconds to let the spices bloom, and then add the tomato paste and diced tomatoes. Season the mixture with salt and stir to combine well.

Deglaze the bottom of the pot by scraping it with a wooden spoon. This is an important step; if the bottom of the pot is not deglazed well, the "burn" error might appear during the pressure-cooking stage. Press the **Cancel** button to turn off the Instant Pot.

Drain the soaked chickpeas and transfer them to the pot, then add 4 cups (960 ml) of water or stock. Taste and adjust the seasonings if needed. Add the kale and the diced potatoes, stirring to combine them with the other ingredients.

Close the Instant Pot's lid and turn the steam-release valve to the sealing position. Press the **Soup/Broth** button and set the timer for 30 minutes at **high pressure**. When the cooking is complete, allow the pressure to release naturally—which will take 15 to 20 minutes—and then open the lid.

Garnish the soup with the cilantro, and then ladle it into bowls. Serve hot with Greek yogurt (if using), slices of red onion, lime wedges and naan (if using).

Note: Chhole masala is readily available in Indian stores or on Amazon. If you can't find it, you can substitute the same amount of Easy Garam Masala (page 172) and ½ of teaspoon of dried mango powder, dried tamarind powder or tamarind concentrate.

Palakachi Patal Bhaji

(Spinach and Buttermilk Soup)

This is a Maharashtrian recipe for cooking spinach in mildly spiced and sweetened buttermilk that is thickened with besan (chickpea flour). Traditionally, it is served with rice, but I love to serve it as soup.

My mom makes the best version of this dish, and I have her make it for me as often as possible when she visits me from India. I tried to replicate my mom's recipe a number of times but just couldn't make it work—until I figured out this foolproof method using the Instant Pot!

Makes 2 servings

1 tbsp (18 g) roasted dalia split (roasted split chickpeas)

1¼ cups (300 ml) water, divided

2 tbsp (18 g) besan (chickpea flour)

2 cups (480 ml) buttermilk, divided

Salt, as needed

1 tsp sugar

2 tbsp (30 ml) neutral oil of choice

¼ cup (37 g) unsalted raw peanuts with skins

½ tsp mustard seeds

½ tsp cumin seeds

½ tsp ground turmeric

¼ tsp asafetida

5 to 6 fresh curry leaves

½-inch (1.3-cm) piece fresh ginger, julienned

1 to 2 green bird's-eye chilies, cut in half lengthwise (optional)

5 oz (140 g) baby spinach (see Variation)

4 to 5 sprigs fresh cilantro, leaves roughly chopped, for garnishing

Sour cream, for serving (optional)

Steamed Ambemohar rice or basmati rice, for serving (optional)

Soak the split chickpeas in ¼ cup (60 ml) of the water for 30 minutes.

Place the chickpea flour in a medium bowl. Stir in ¼ cup (60 ml) of the buttermilk. Whisk to form a smooth paste, and then gently pour in the remaining 1¾ cups (420 ml) of buttermilk. This will ensure that there are no lumps in the mixture. Add the remaining 1 cup (240 ml) of water, salt and sugar and whisk well to combine the ingredients.

Place the inner pot in the Instant Pot and press the **Sauté** button. When the display reads "Hot," add the oil and peanuts. Fry the peanuts for 2 to 3 minutes, until the skins turn a slightly darker shade of brown. Using a slotted spoon, remove the peanuts from the pot and set them aside on a plate lined with paper towels, so that they can drain. Alternatively, you can leave the peanuts in the pot after frying them and let them cook in the soup.

Add the mustard seeds, cumin seeds, turmeric and asafetida. When the seeds sizzle and the turmeric and asafetida froth, add the curry leaves, ginger and bird's-eye chilies (if using). Stir in the split chickpeas along with the soaking water.

Sauté the mixture for 1 minute, and then add the spinach. Sauté the mixture for 2 minutes, until the spinach wilts. Press the **Cancel** button. Pour in the flour-buttermilk mixture and stir to combine everything.

Close the Instant Pot's lid and turn the steam-release valve to the sealing position. Press the **Soup/Broth** button and set the timer for 10 minutes. Then press the **Pressure** button to change the pressure to **low**. When the cooking is complete, let the pressure release naturally—which will take 10 to 12 minutes—and then open the lid. Taste and adjust the seasonings if needed.

Ladle the soup into bowls. Top the soup with the cilantro, sour cream (if using) and fried peanuts and serve it hot. Alternatively, you can serve the soup over a bed of steamed rice (if using).

Variation: Substitute the spinach with chopped rainbow or Swiss chard, baby kale or collard greens for a change.

Manchow Soup

(Chicken and Vegetable Soup)

Manchow soup is originally from the eastern state of Meghalaya but is popular all over India, and it's my absolute favorite! I like to think of it as a hot and spicy Indian version of Chinese egg drop soup, and its volume is turned up with chicken and vegetables. I simply dump the chicken and vegetables in the Instant Pot, along with the seasonings and the stock, to cook everything together. This way the chicken gets a chance to absorb all the amazing flavors as it is cooked in the seasoned broth.

Serves 4 to 6

2 tbsp (30 ml) neutral oil of choice

1 small jalapeño, deseeded and minced

5 to 6 cloves garlic, minced

1-inch (2.5-cm) piece fresh ginger, finely grated

10 to 12 haricot verts (French green beans), trimmed and thinly sliced

1 small carrot, finely chopped

1 cup (100 g) finely chopped cabbage

½ tsp finely ground black pepper

Salt, as needed

8 cups (1.9 L) chicken stock

¼ cup (60 ml) soy sauce

1 lb (454 g) bone-in, skinless chicken breast (see Variations)

⅓ cup (43 g) cornstarch

⅔ cup (160 ml) water

1 large egg

8 to 10 sprigs fresh cilantro, leaves minced, for garnishing

1 medium green onion, thinly sliced, for garnishing

Fresh bean sprouts, for garnishing (optional)

Fried noodles (such as chow mein noodles), for garnishing (optional)

Szechuan Chutney (page 168), for serving (optional)

Place the inner pot in the Instant Pot and press the **Sauté** button. When the display reads "Hot," add the oil, jalapeño, garlic and ginger. Sauté the mixture for 1 minute, and then stir in the haricot verts, carrot and cabbage. Sauté the vegetables for 2 minutes, and then season them with the black pepper and salt. Press the **Cancel** button and sauté the vegetables for 1 minute on the residual heat.

Pour in the chicken stock and soy sauce and stir to combine the ingredients. Place the chicken breast in the seasoned stock, making sure it is fully immersed.

Close the Instant Pot's lid and turn the steam-release valve to the sealing position. Press the **Soup/Broth** button and set the timer for 10 minutes at **high pressure**. When the cooking is complete, allow the pressure to release naturally—which will take 20 to 25 minutes—and then open the lid. Press the **Cancel** button.

Using a pair of tongs or a slotted spoon, gently transfer the chicken breast to a medium bowl or deep platter. Using two forks, shred the cooked chicken. Discard the bones and return the shredded meat to the stock in the pot.

In a small bowl, combine the cornstarch and water. Whisk the mixture well to form a slurry, ensuring there are no lumps. Pour the slurry into the soup. Press the **Sauté** button and bring the soup to a boil.

In the meantime, crack the egg into a small bowl and whisk it. Once the soup comes to a boil, gently pour in the egg and stir the soup continuously for about 1 minute, until the soup has thickened and the egg has cooked. Press the **Cancel** button.

Ladle the soup into bowls and serve it hot, garnished with the cilantro, green onion, bean sprouts (if using) and fried noodles (if using). Stir in a bit of the Szechuan Chutney (if using) for a spicy kick.

Variations

• Add other finely chopped vegetables, like bell peppers, mushrooms or riced cauliflower.

• Make it vegan by substituting the chicken with tofu and the chicken stock with vegetable stock, skipping the egg and using a vegan variety of fried noodles.

Saar

(Spicy Tomato Soup)

Saar, the Maharashtrian spicy soup, is a delicious, light, brothy soup made mainly with tomatoes but also with vegetables like carrots, potatoes or even beets. It is spiced with fresh coconut paste and seasoned with spices and curry leaves. The sweetness from the coconut in the paste balances out the tanginess of the tomatoes and the spiciness from the chilies, making this soup lip-smackingly delicious!

There are a couple of versions of the recipe, one with the addition of roasted peanuts in the paste and another with the addition of coconut milk to thicken the soup. It is usually slurped on its own but can also be served with rice on the side or paired with Masale Bhaat (page 100).

Serves 2 to 4

Soup Base

4 medium tomatoes, quartered

1 small Yukon gold potato, halved (see Variations)

1 medium carrot, roughly chopped

1½ cups (360 ml) water

4 to 5 black peppercorns

½-inch (1.3-cm) piece cinnamon bark

1 dried bay leaf

Paste

¼ cup (4 g) roughly chopped fresh cilantro leaves and tender stems

¼ cup (25 g) grated fresh or thawed frozen coconut

1 to 2 green bird's-eye chilies, broken into pieces (optional)

2 cloves garlic, smashed and peeled

½-inch (1.3-cm) piece fresh ginger, peeled

Start by making the soup base. Place the tomatoes, potato, carrot, water, peppercorns, cinnamon bark and bay leaf in the inner pot of the Instant Pot. Close the Instant Pot's lid and turn the steam-release valve to the sealing position. Press the **Manual/Pressure Cook** button and set the timer for 5 minutes at **high pressure**. When the cooking is complete, allow the pressure to release naturally—which will take 12 to 15 minutes—and then open the lid.

Take the inner pot out of the Instant Pot. Set the inner pot aside and let the cooked vegetables cool for 15 to 20 minutes.

In the meantime, make the paste. In a blender or food processor, combine the cilantro, coconut, bird's-eye chilies (if using), garlic and ginger. Process the ingredients to a smooth paste. Set aside.

Once the vegetables have cooled, transfer them and their cooking liquid to a blender. Puree the vegetables until they are smooth. Strain the puree through a sieve and set it aside. Rinse the inner pot and wipe it dry.

(continued)

Rajma Chawal *(continued)*

4 to 5 sprigs fresh cilantro, leaves roughly chopped, for garnishing

1 medium green onion, thinly sliced, for garnishing

Thickly sliced red onion, for serving (optional)

Green bird's-eye chilies, serrano chilies or jalapeño chilies, for serving (optional)

Close the Instant Pot's lid and turn the steam-release valve to the sealing position. Press the **Bean/Chili** button and set the timer for 40 minutes at **high pressure**. When the cooking is complete, allow the pressure to release naturally—which will take 15 to 20 minutes—and then open the lid. Note that older or traditional kidney beans take longer to cook. If you find that your beans are not soft and haven't cooked all the way through, close the lid immediately and set the Instant Pot to cook using the **Bean/Chili** mode for another 10 minutes at **high pressure**. After the cooking is complete, allow the pressure to release naturally before opening the lid.

Garnish the beans and rice with the cilantro and green onion. Ladle the beans and rice into bowls and serve them with slices of red onion (if using) and bird's-eye chilies (if using).

Notes:

• I recommend using the Jammu or Kashmiri rajma or red kidney beans that are readily available in Indian stores. They are smaller in size and cook faster compared to the traditional dark red kidney beans.

• Rajma masala is available in Indian stores or on Amazon or other online stores. Read more about it on page 183. If you cannot find it, you can substitute it with the same amount of Easy Garam Masala (page 172) combined with 1 teaspoon kasuri methi (dried fenugreek leaves) and ¼ teaspoon dried mango powder, dried tamarind powder or tamarind concentrate.

Variations

• For added nutrition, mix in 2 cups (134 g) of chopped kale or spinach along with the beans and rice and allow them to cook together.

• Replace the red kidney beans with black or pinto beans for variation.

Simple Stews and Humble Veggies

Having grown up a vegetarian, I tend to fall back on simple stews and humble veggies more often than any meat-based dish. As I was growing up, Mom put a delightful and wholesome vegetarian meal on our plates every single day. There was a quick vegetable stir-fry or a curry like Bharli Dodaki (Stuffed Ridge Gourd Curry; page 78). Or she would fill the family up with a hearty dal or bean stew, like Usal (Baby Lima Bean Stew; page 74), along with hot chapatis off the flame, steamed rice and a refreshing side salad. Those were the days! While it is not realistic for me to put that kind of meal together after work on weeknights, thanks to the Instant Pot, I am able to whip up delicious and healthy home-cooked meals, like a stew or vegetable curry and rice or quinoa, cooked pot-in-pot.

After a long day at work, I crave a restaurant favorite that I can make at home faster than I can order takeout—Kadhai Paneer (Indian Cottage Cheese in Spiced Tomato Sauce; page 68)—and that gets the family excited about dinnertime. And Mushroom Caldine (Mushrooms in Coconut Milk Curry; page 71) can strike up a great dinner conversation about one of our best vacations in Goa! Then there's Mumma's Dal Fry (Mixed Lentil Stew; page 64) that I run to if I'm in need of a tight, comforting hug. I relive delicious childhood memories and think of my grandmoms by making the spicy and tangy Tomato Batata Rassa (Tomatoes and Potatoes in Spiced Peanut Broth; page 81) or hearty legume stews like the Amti (Split Pigeon Pea Stew; page 67) and Hirva Kolambu (Red Lentil Stew with Herbed Coconut Paste; page 77).

Most of the recipes in this chapter are traditional, from my beloved Maharashtrian culture and heritage. They are family recipes that were handed down to me and have a special place in my heart. I hope you love them as much as I do!

Mumma's Dal Fry

(Mixed Lentil Stew)

Whenever my parents visit, my mom takes over my kitchen and cooks all of my favorite foods including her signature dal fry! Mom makes this dish with seven different beans and lentils cooked together and then stir-fries them with lots of garlic mixed with spiced onions and tomatoes. Spooned over basmati rice, it's like Mom giving my husband and me a comforting hug!

Serves 4

¼ cup (50 g) toor dal (dried split pigeon peas)

¼ cup (50 g) yellow moong dal (dried split moong beans)

¼ cup (50 g) masoor dal (dried split red lentils)

2 tbsp (25 g) moong chilka (dried split green gram with husk)

2 tbsp (25 g) chana dal (dried split chickpeas)

2 tbsp (25 g) urad chilka (dried split black gram with husks)

2 tbsp (25 g) urad gota (dried black gram without husks)

2 tbsp (30 ml) neutral oil of choice

1 tsp cumin seeds

¼ tsp asafetida

5 to 6 fresh curry leaves

1 to 2 dried spicy red chilies (optional)

4 to 5 cloves garlic, roughly chopped

1 small onion, thickly sliced

2 small tomatoes, thickly sliced

½ tsp ground turmeric

Salt, as needed

½ tsp sugar

4 cups (960 ml) water

4 large leaves rainbow or Swiss chard, stems trimmed and roughly chopped (see Variations)

8 to 10 sprigs fresh cilantro, leaves roughly chopped, for garnishing

1 medium green onion, thinly sliced, for garnishing

Rinse the pigeon peas, moong beans, red lentils, green gram, split chickpeas, black gram with husks and black gram without husks together in a sieve under cold tap water until the water runs clear. Set the rinsed dals aside.

Place the inner pot in the Instant Pot and press the **Sauté** button. When the display reads "Hot," add the oil, cumin seeds and asafetida. When the seeds sizzle and the asafetida froths, add the curry leaves, red chilies (if using) and garlic. Sauté for 30 seconds, and then stir in the onion. Mix well and sauté for 2 to 3 minutes, until the onion softens a bit.

Stir in the tomatoes. Season the mixture with the turmeric, salt and sugar. Sauté the mixture for 2 minutes, until the tomatoes soften and release their moisture. Press the **Cancel** button.

Add the rinsed dal mixture, and then pour in the water. Stir well to combine the ingredients. Taste the water and adjust the salt level if needed. Close the Instant Pot's lid and turn the steam-release valve to the sealing position. Press the **Bean/Chili** button, and then press the **Adjust** button to set the timer for 15 minutes at **high pressure**. When the cooking is complete, open the lid using a quick pressure release to depressurize the Instant Pot.

Stir in the chard. Close the lid and let the stew warm for 15 to 20 minutes, or until you are ready to serve it, so that the chard wilts and the flavors develop.

Garnish the stew with the cilantro and green onion and serve it warm.

Variations

• Substitute rainbow or Swiss chard with any other leafy greens like spinach, baby kale or collard greens.

• You can use any number and/or combination of dals that you may have on hand but make sure to maintain the proportion of toor, masoor and moong dals higher than the other dals you may use.

Amti

(Split Pigeon Pea Stew)

Amti, a hearty stew of split pigeon peas, is integral in Marathi households. It is mildly spiced with goda masala and gets its sweet and sour flavor from the chincha (tamarind) and gul (jaggery).

Growing up, I ate this dish daily, and Mom would switch it up with different ingredients, like baby eggplant, fenugreek leaves or—one of my absolute favorites—shevgyachya shenga (moringa pods), commonly known as drumsticks. It is my ajji's (maternal grandmother's) signature concoction! I have fond memories of picking the drumsticks from the tree near her farmhouse, but now I just get fresh or frozen ones from my Indian grocery store.

Serves 3 to 4

5 to 6 moringa pods (see Variations)

¾ cup (150 g) toor dal (dried split pigeon peas)

2 tbsp (30 ml) neutral oil of choice

½ tsp mustard seeds (see Variations)

½ tsp ground turmeric

¼ tsp asafetida

5 to 6 fresh curry leaves

Salt, as needed

2 tsp (4 g) Quick Goda Masala (page 175)

3 cups (720 ml) water

1 tsp tamarind concentrate

1 tbsp (10 g) powdered jaggery or coconut palm sugar

4 to 5 sprigs fresh cilantro, leaves roughly chopped, for garnishing

Steamed Ambemohar rice or basmati rice, for serving

Wash the moringa pods and trim the ends. Cut each pod into 3-inch (8-cm)-long pieces and set them aside.

Rinse the pigeon peas in a sieve under cold tap water until the water runs clear. Set the pigeon peas aside.

Place the inner pot in the Instant Pot and press the **Sauté** button. When the display reads "Hot," add the oil, mustard seeds, turmeric and asafetida. When the seeds sizzle and the turmeric and asafetida froth, add the curry leaves and moringa pods. Season the mixture with salt, and then add the Quick Goda Masala. Sauté the mixture for 1 to 2 minutes. Press the **Cancel** button.

Add the pigeon peas and pour in the water. Stir in the tamarind concentrate and powdered jaggery and mix everything together well.

Close the Instant Pot's lid and turn the steam-release valve to the sealing position. Press the **Manual/Pressure Cook** button and set the timer for 10 minutes at **high pressure**. When the cooking is complete, allow the pressure to release naturally—which will take 12 to 15 minutes—and then open the lid.

Garnish the stew with the cilantro and serve it hot spooned over the rice.

Variations

- Add in ½ teaspoon of methi or fenugreek seeds along with mustard seeds for a different flavor.

- Substitute the moringa pods with:

  - quartered baby eggplant or fresh fenugreek leaves; decrease the cooking time to 6 minutes.

  - baby spinach; decrease the cooking time to 6 minutes and add the baby spinach after the cooking is complete, then keep the stew warm for 15 to 20 minutes, until the spinach wilts.

  - a small diced onion; sauté the onion for 5 minutes, until it is translucent, before adding the pigeon peas and water.

Kadhai Paneer

(Indian Cottage Cheese in Spiced Tomato Sauce)

Kadhai paneer, a popular vegetarian item on the menus of Indian restaurants, is made by stir-frying cubes of paneer cheese and bell peppers with a spicy onion-tomato masala sauce in a special Indian wok called a kadhai. Garnished with julienned ginger, this dish pairs very well with naan or basmati rice.

The masala sauce gets its distinctive flavor from a special spice blend, called kadhai masala, that is made by crushing coriander seeds, black peppercorns and red pepper flakes together with a mortar and pestle. The Instant Pot does a fantastic job pressure-cooking the sauce. It comes out tasting just like it does when it's cooked in the kadhai—and you don't have to do any stir-frying with a hot wok!

Serves 4

1 tbsp (6 g) coriander seeds

½ to 1 tsp red pepper flakes

½ tsp black peppercorns

3 tbsp (45 ml) neutral oil of choice, divided

2 large bell peppers (any color or mixture of colors), cut into 1-inch (2.5-cm) cubes

1 small onion, cut into 1-inch (2.5-cm) cubes

1-inch (2.5-cm) piece cinnamon bark

2 to 3 pods green cardamom

1 tsp cumin seeds

¼ tsp asafetida

1 medium onion, minced

Salt, as needed

½-inch (1.3-cm) piece fresh ginger, minced

2 cloves garlic, finely grated

½ tsp ground turmeric

½ tbsp (3 g) Kashmiri red chili powder

1 tbsp (16 g) tomato paste

3 medium tomatoes, pureed

Using a mortar and pestle or a spice grinder, grind together the coriander seeds, red pepper flakes and peppercorns until a coarse powder forms—this is the kadhai masala. Set the masala aside.

Place the inner pot in the Instant Pot and press the **Sauté** button. When the display reads "Hot," add 1 tablespoon (15 ml) of the oil. Transfer the cubed bell peppers and cubed onion to the pot and lightly fry them for 2 minutes, stirring them continuously, until they are lightly charred in a few spots. Remove the pepper-onion mixture from the pot and set it aside.

Add the remaining 2 tablespoons (30 ml) of oil, cinnamon bark, green cardamom pods, cumin seeds and asafetida. When the whole spices sizzle and the asafetida froths, add the minced onion. Season the onion with salt to help it soften. Sauté the mixture for 5 to 7 minutes, stirring it frequently, until the onion is translucent.

Stir in the minced ginger and the garlic. Sauté the mixture for 1 minute. Stir in the kadhai masala, then add the turmeric and Kashmiri red chili powder. Sauté the mixture for about 30 seconds to let the spices bloom, and then add the tomato paste and the pureed tomatoes. Season the mixture with additional salt and stir to combine the ingredients well. Deglaze the bottom of the pot by scraping it with a wooden spoon. This is an important step; if the bottom of the pot is not deglazed well, the "burn" error might appear during the pressure-cooking stage.

Cook the mixture for 5 minutes, until the tomatoes lose most of their moisture. Press the **Cancel** button to turn off the Instant Pot.

(continued)

Mushroom Caldine *(continued)*

4 to 5 sprigs fresh cilantro, leaves roughly chopped, for garnishing

For Serving

Steamed basmati rice

Thickly sliced red onion (optional)

Green bird's-eye chilies, serrano chilies or jalapeño chilies (optional)

Lime or lemon wedges (optional)

Open the lid, garnish the curry with the cilantro and serve it hot with the rice, red onion (if using), bird's-eye chilies (if using) and lime wedges (if using) on the side.

Note: If you prefer a milder flavor, you can use fewer red chilies or omit them entirely.

Variations

• You can substitute mushrooms with cauliflower, okra or bottle gourd. Use the same pressure-cooking time as you would for mushrooms, but depressurize the Instant Pot using a quick pressure release.

• You can use any firm whitefish or shrimp in place of mushrooms in the recipe. Use the same pressure-cooking time as you would for mushrooms, but change the pressure setting to **low pressure** and depressurize the Instant Pot using a quick pressure release.

Usal

(Baby Lima Bean Stew)

Maharashtrian cuisine has a repertoire of stews made with a variety of beans, sprouted or dried, called usal (pronounced "oo-sal"). Growing up, I ate all the kinds that Mom would make, but my absolute favorite was and still is the vaalachi usal: field or hyacinth bean stew in a mild coconut broth.

While this stew is easy to make, it usually needs some advanced planning—about 72 hours—as the beans need to be soaked, sprouted and peeled before making the stew. So I found a shortcut! I use dried baby lima beans, which can be cooked directly in the Instant Pot without soaking! The addition of dill gives the stew the characteristic mellow, bitter flavor that comes from the vaal beans.

Serves 4

1 cup (175 g) dried baby lima beans (see Variations)

2 tbsp (30 ml) neutral oil of choice

½ tsp mustard seeds

½ tsp ground turmeric

¼ tsp asafetida

5 to 6 fresh curry leaves

Salt, as needed

2 tsp (4 g) Quick Goda Masala (page 175)

Red chili powder, as needed (optional)

1 tbsp (10 g) packed powdered jaggery or coconut palm sugar

2 tbsp (6 g) finely chopped fresh dill

½ cup (50 g) grated fresh or thawed frozen coconut

1½ cups (360 ml) water

4 to 5 sprigs fresh cilantro, leaves roughly chopped, for garnishing

Whole wheat chapatis or phulka rotis, for serving

Steamed basmati rice or cooked quinoa, for serving (optional)

Radishes, for serving (optional)

Baby cucumbers, cut into sticks, for serving (optional)

Indian pickles, for serving (optional; see Note)

Sort through the lima beans, removing any small stones and malformed or damaged beans. Rinse the beans under cold tap water.

Place the inner pot in the Instant Pot and press the **Sauté** button. When the display reads "Hot," add the oil, mustard seeds, turmeric and asafetida.

When the seeds sizzle and the turmeric and asafetida froth, add the curry leaves and lima beans. Sauté the mixture for 1 minute. Press the **Cancel** button to turn off the Instant Pot.

Season the mixture with the salt, Quick Goda Masala and red chili powder (if using). Stir in the powdered jaggery, dill, coconut and water. Mix well.

Close the Instant Pot's lid and turn the steam-release valve to the sealing position. Press the **Bean/Chili** button and set the timer for 30 minutes at **high pressure**. When the cooking is complete, allow the pressure to release naturally—which will take 12 to 15 minutes—and then open the lid.

Garnish the stew with the cilantro. Serve it hot along with the chapatis, basmati rice (if using), radishes (if using), cucumbers (if using) and Indian pickles (if using).

Note: Indian pickles—like green mangoes, green chilies, limes or a mixed variety—are available in Indian grocery stores.

Variations

• Substitute baby lima beans with black-eyed peas.

• Stir in chopped spinach or baby kale after the cooking is complete and keep the stew warm for 15 to 20 minutes, until the greens wilt.

Hirva Kolambu

(Red Lentil Stew with Herbed Coconut Paste)

Growing up in a joint family, I had two grandmothers in the house: One was my dad's mom and the other was my dad's aunt, Didi. Didi was originally from Karnataka, one of the states in the southern part of India, and she passed down all of our family recipes to my mom, along with quite a few of her traditional Kannada recipes. This recipe of cooking dal with snake gourd and spicing it with an herbed coconut paste, hirva masala, is one of her Kannada signature concoctions.

Serves 4 to 6

Hirva Masala (See Variations)

22 to 25 sprigs fresh cilantro, leaves and tender stems roughly chopped

¾ cup (75 g) grated fresh or thawed frozen coconut

4 to 5 green bird's-eye chilies, broken into pieces (use fewer or omit for less spice)

1-inch (2.5-cm) piece fresh ginger, peeled

1 tsp cumin seeds

¼ cup (60 ml) water

Stew

1 large snake gourd (see Variations)

¾ cup (150 g) masoor dal (split red lentils; see Variations)

2 tbsp (30 ml) neutral oil of choice

½ tsp mustard seeds

½ tsp ground turmeric

¼ tsp asafetida

Salt, as needed

3 cups (720 ml) water

1 tsp tamarind concentrate (or substitute with juice from ½ lemon or lime)

4 to 5 sprigs fresh cilantro, leaves roughly chopped, for garnishing

For Serving

Steamed Sona Masuri rice or basmati rice

Spicy Indian pickles (optional)

To make the hirva masala, combine the cilantro, coconut, bird's-eye chilies, ginger, cumin seeds and water in a blender or food processor. Blend the ingredients until they form a smooth paste. Set the hirva masala aside.

To make the stew, wash and trim the ends of the gourd. Cut it into about 4-inch (10-cm)-long pieces, so that it's easier to handle. Slice each piece in half lengthwise and scoop out and discard the white flesh and seeds. Cut each piece into ¼-inch (6-mm)-thick slices. Set the slices of gourd aside.

Rinse the red lentils under cold tap water until the water runs clear. Set aside.

Place the inner pot in the Instant Pot and press the **Sauté** button. When the display reads "Hot," add the oil, mustard seeds, turmeric and asafetida. When the seeds sizzle and the turmeric and asafetida froth, add the gourd. Season them with salt and sauté the gourd for 30 seconds. Press the **Cancel** button.

Add in the lentils and pour in the water. Stir in the hirva masala and tamarind concentrate, and mix well. Close the Instant Pot's lid and turn the steam-release valve to the sealing position. Press the **Manual/Pressure Cook** button and set the timer for 6 minutes at **high pressure**. When the cooking is complete, allow the pressure to release naturally—which will take 12 to 15 minutes—and then open the lid.

Gently stir the stew to combine everything, making sure the gourd slices stay intact. Garnish the stew with the cilantro and serve it hot spooned over the rice along with the Indian pickles (if using) on the side.

> *Variations*
> - Substitute snake gourd with ridge gourd, bottle gourd or chayote squash.
> - You can use whole brown or green lentils or even toor dal (split pigeon peas) instead of masoor dal.
> - The hirva masala is great in other onion-tomato or coconut milk–based curries that include chicken, fish or seafood.

Bharli Dodaki

(Stuffed Ridge Gourd Curry)

Dodaka or turai, commonly known as ridge gourd or Chinese okra, was a regular in my house while I was growing up. My mom makes a delicious curry by stuffing gourd chunks with crushed roasted peanuts, powdered jaggery, red chili powder and the Maharashtrian goda masala. The traditional curry needs to simmer on the stove for a while so that the thick and tough skin of the gourd can cook, making it perfect for cooking under pressure in the Instant Pot. With its wonderful contrast of flavors and textures, this hot and sweet curry is out of this world!

Serves 4

Stuffing

2 medium ridge gourds, ends trimmed and ridges peeled (see Variations)

¼ cup (37 g) unsalted roasted peanuts, coarsely ground

¼ cup (40 g) ground jaggery or coconut palm sugar

Red chili powder, as needed

1 tbsp (6 g) Quick Goda Masala (page 175)

Salt, as needed

Curry

2 tbsp (30 ml) neutral oil of choice

½ tsp mustard seeds

½ tsp ground turmeric

¼ tsp asafetida

½ cup (120 ml) water

2 tbsp (13 g) grated fresh or thawed frozen coconut, for garnishing

4 to 5 sprigs fresh cilantro, leaves roughly chopped, for garnishing

For Serving

Chapatis or phulka rotis (optional)

Steamed Ambemohar rice or basmati rice (optional)

Begin by preparing the stuffing. Cut each gourd into 1-inch (2.5-cm)-long pieces. Slit each piece open lengthwise, being careful not to cut all the way through the gourd pieces, as they will need to hold the stuffing. Set aside.

In a small bowl, combine the peanuts, jaggery, red chili powder, Quick Goda Masala and salt. Mix well. Stuff the pieces of ridge gourd by opening the slit and filling it with about ½ tablespoon (8 g) of the stuffing mixture. Set aside. Reserve any unused stuffing mixture.

To make the curry, place the inner pot in the Instant Pot and press the **Sauté** button. When the display reads "Hot," add the oil, mustard seeds, turmeric and asafetida. When the seeds sizzle and the turmeric and asafetida froth, add the stuffed gourd pieces. Press the **Cancel** button.

Stir the gourd pieces to coat them with the spiced oil. Add the water and stir everything gently. Add any leftover stuffing and stir to combine.

Close the Instant Pot's lid and turn the steam-release valve to the sealing position. Press the **Manual/Pressure Cook** button and set the timer for 4 minutes at **high pressure**. When the cooking is complete, allow the pressure to release naturally—which will take 9 to 11 minutes—and then open the lid.

Press the **Cancel** button and then immediately press the **Sauté** button to cook off some of the excess moisture. The curry will come to a gentle boil. Stir occasionally, making sure the gourd chunks don't break apart. Press the **Cancel** button.

Garnish the curry with the coconut and cilantro. Serve it hot with the chapatis (if using) or rice (if using).

Variations

• Don't like the ridge gourd? Use baby eggplants or okra instead. Use the same settings for time and pressure, but when the cooking is complete, open the lid using a quick pressure release.

• You can add ¼ cup (25 g) of grated fresh or thawed frozen coconut to the stuffing mixture.

Tomato Batata Rassa

(Tomatoes and Potatoes in Spiced Peanut Broth)

While I didn't really see my paternal grandmother step into the kitchen when we kids were little, there were some of her signature concoctions that she shared with my mom, who passed them down to me. This humble stew, made with the most basic ingredients—tomatoes and potatoes that are simmered together in a spicy broth thickened with ground roasted peanuts—was one of those.

I've adapted my grandmother's recipe for the Instant Pot. I use grape or cherry tomatoes and tiny potatoes, and I've added baby spinach as well. I simply dump all the ingredients in the pot, and the dish is ready in just a few minutes! Spooned over steamed basmati rice, it's a quick, healthy and comforting meal.

Serves 2 to 3

2 tbsp (30 ml) neutral oil of choice

½ tsp cumin seeds

½ tsp mustard seeds

½ tsp ground turmeric

¼ tsp asafetida

8 oz (224 g) grape or cherry tomatoes

8 oz (224 g) baby potatoes (see Variations)

Salt, as needed

Red chili powder, as needed (optional)

1 tsp packed powdered jaggery or coconut palm sugar

2 tbsp (18 g) unsalted roasted peanuts, coarsely ground

2 tbsp (12 g) grated fresh or thawed frozen coconut

¾ cup (180 ml) water (see Variations)

2 cups (60 g) baby spinach

Steamed Ambemohar rice, basmati rice or cooked quinoa, for serving

Whole wheat chapatis or phulka rotis, for serving

Place the inner pot in the Instant Pot and press the **Sauté** button. When the display reads "Hot," add the oil, cumin seeds, mustard seeds, turmeric and asafetida. When the seeds sizzle and the turmeric and asafetida froth, add the tomatoes and potatoes. Sauté the mixture for 1 minute. Press the **Cancel** button.

Season the mixture with salt and red chili powder (if using). Stir in the jaggery, peanuts, coconut and water. Mix everything together well.

Close the Instant Pot's lid and turn the steam-release valve to the sealing position.

Press the **Manual/Pressure Cook** button and set the timer for 5 minutes at **high pressure**. When cooking is complete, allow the pressure to release naturally—which will take about 15 minutes—and then open the lid.

Press the **Cancel** button, then add the baby spinach.

Press the **Sauté** button. Gently stir the mixture, making sure not to mash the tomatoes, and bring it to a boil so that the spinach wilts. This should take 4 to 5 minutes. Press the **Cancel** button.

Spoon the tomato batata rassa over the rice and serve it warm with the whole wheat chapatis.

Variations

• Substitute baby potatoes with sweet potatoes, bottle gourd or butternut squash.

• Add cooked chickpeas for added protein.

• Stir in some shrimp along with the baby spinach for added protein.

• Substitute ¼ cup (60 ml) of the water with ¼ cup (60 ml) of coconut milk to thicken the broth.

For Fish and Seafood *Fans*

It's very unlike me, but a few years ago, I went through a phase when I just didn't care for poultry or meat and instead got into fish and seafood. I went as far as declaring myself to be a pescatarian—if you were in front of me right now, you'd see me roll my eyes at myself. Even though I'm no longer in that phase, I still find myself going for fish and seafood whenever I get a chance, because it's lighter and healthier compared to meat and has more protein compared to vegetarian or vegan options.

It helps that my husband and daughter are fish and seafood fans like me. I love to whip up our favorite spicy seafood curries like the Mangalorean Yeti Gassi (Shrimp in Tangy Coconut Curry; page 84) or the Maharashtrian Tisaryache Kalvan (Clams in Green Mango and Coconut Curry; page 95) on weeknights or weekends. When my grocery haul includes salmon or halibut fillets, it's Bengali-style Bhapa Shorshe Maach (Steamed Mustard Salmon; page 90) or Keralan Meen Moilee (Halibut Poached in Spiced Coconut Milk Broth; page 87) for a weeknight dinner or weekend brunch. During crab season, I have to make the Crab Xacuti (Crab in Spicy Coconut Curry; page 93), which takes my family back to our most memorable vacation in Goa. The dishes in this chapter are typically served as a main course with steamed basmati rice on the side.

Cooking fish and seafood on the stove can be tricky, as it can overcook in the blink of an eye! I find the Instant Pot to be more consistent and reliable when it comes to cooking fish or seafood to perfection.

Yeti Gassi

(Shrimp in Tangy Coconut Curry)

Gassi is a spicy Mangalorean curry from the state of Karnataka that gets its heat from the use of locally grown Byadgi chilies and its tanginess from another local ingredient called jaargey, the dried skin of a fruit. Jaargey is not easily available and can be substituted with kokum, or wild mangosteen (read more about kokum on page 182). It is a very versatile curry and is used as a base for meat, poultry, vegetables or fish and seafood.

The gassi masala paste is made by grinding raw onion along with coconut and spices. It needs to be cooked thoroughly; otherwise, the taste can be quite unpleasant. Thankfully, pressure-cooking it in the Instant Pot is way faster than simmering it on the stove.

Serves 3 to 4

Gassi Masala
½ medium onion, roughly chopped

½ cup (50 g) grated fresh or thawed frozen coconut

10 to 12 dried red Byadgi/Bedgi chilies, broken into pieces (see Notes)

1 tbsp (6 g) coriander seeds

¼ tsp fenugreek seeds

½ tsp black peppercorns

5 to 6 cloves garlic, peeled

1-inch (2.5-cm) piece fresh ginger, roughly chopped

1 cup (240 ml) water

Begin with making the gassi masala. In a high-powered blender or food grinder, combine the onion, coconut, Byadgi chilies, coriander, fenugreek seeds, peppercorns, garlic, ginger and water. Blend the ingredients until they form a fine, smooth paste.

Notes:
• Byadgi chilies are moderately spicy, with a vibrant red color. They are readily available in Indian stores or online on Amazon. If you can't find them, you can substitute with Kashmiri red chilies, either in whole or ground form. If you use ground chili powder, I recommend using 1 tablespoon (6 g).

• Kokum (wild mangosteen) is readily available in Indian stores or online on Amazon. There are two varieties: dry and wet. Either variety will work in this recipe. If you cannot find kokum, you can substitute it with 1 teaspoon of tamarind concentrate or the juice from half of a medium lime.

Variations
• Make it vegan by substituting the shrimp with cauliflower, potatoes or cooked chickpeas.

• Substitute the shrimp with cubed boneless, skinless chicken thighs to make kori gassi. Add the cubed chicken to the sauce and pressure-cook the chicken and the sauce together according to the directions in the recipe.

(continued)

Yeti Gassi *(continued)*

Curry

2 tbsp (30 ml) melted coconut oil or neutral oil of choice

½ tsp mustard seeds

½ tsp cumin seeds

¼ tsp asafetida

5 to 6 fresh curry leaves

½ medium onion, finely chopped

Salt, as needed

½ tsp ground turmeric

1½ cups (360 ml) water

5 to 6 kokum petals (see Notes)

½ tsp sugar

8 oz (224 g) medium shrimp, peeled, deveined and tails removed (see Variations)

4 to 5 sprigs fresh cilantro, leaves roughly chopped, for garnishing

For Serving

Steamed Sona Masuri rice or basmati rice

Neer dosas (recommended), whole wheat chapatis or phulka rotis

To make the curry, place the inner pot in the Instant Pot and press the **Sauté** button. When the display reads "Hot," add the coconut oil, mustard seeds, cumin seeds, asafetida and curry leaves. When the curry leaves splutter, add the onion. Season the mixture with salt to help the onion soften. Sauté the mixture for about 5 minutes, stirring it frequently, until the onion is translucent.

Add the turmeric and sauté the mixture for about 30 seconds to let the turmeric bloom. Stir in the gassi masala and sauté the mixture for 5 to 7 minutes, stirring it frequently, until the mixture doesn't smell raw anymore.

Press the **Cancel** button to turn off the Instant Pot.

Pour in the water and add the kokum petals. Season the mixture with the sugar and additional salt if needed. Stir the ingredients well to combine them.

Close the Instant Pot's lid and turn the steam-release valve to the sealing position. Press the **Manual/Pressure Cook** button and set the timer for 10 minutes at **high pressure**. When the cooking is complete, allow the pressure to release naturally—which will take 12 to 15 minutes—and then open the lid.

Add the shrimp to the pot. Stir the curry to combine the ingredients and close the lid. Let the curry sit, undisturbed, for about 10 minutes to allow the shrimp to cook. You may need to adjust the time, depending on the size of the shrimp. If you are using a smaller size, decrease the time by about 2 minutes; if you are using larger shrimp, add about 2 minutes to allow them to cook well.

Garnish the curry with the cilantro and serve it hot with the rice and neer dosas.

Meen Moilee

(Halibut Poached in Spiced Coconut Milk Broth)

Meen moilee is a classic Kerala-style fish curry made by poaching the fish in a light, moderately spicy, curry leaf–scented coconut milk broth. It's a vibrant yellow curry that gets its gorgeous color from turmeric, which is used in both the marinade and the base. Sliced jalapeño adds a hint of heat that is balanced out with the sweetness from the coconut milk and the tanginess from lemon juice. Spooned over rice, appam or idiappam, this dish makes for a quick and easy weeknight dinner or an elegant and traditional weekend brunch.

Before the Instant Pot, I overcooked the fish several times when making this recipe. But after I tried the recipe in the Instant Pot, I haven't gone back to making it on the stove!

Serves 3 to 4

Halibut

4 (4-oz [112-g], 1-inch [2.5-cm]-thick) halibut fillets or fish fillets of choice (see Variations)

Juice of ½ medium lemon or lime

½ tsp ground turmeric

½ tsp finely ground black pepper

Salt, as needed

Spiced Coconut Milk Broth

2 tbsp (30 ml) melted coconut oil or neutral oil of choice

5 to 6 fresh curry leaves

½ tsp mustard seeds

¼ tsp asafetida

1 small onion, thinly sliced

Salt, as needed

½-inch (1.3-cm) piece fresh ginger, finely grated

2 cloves garlic, finely grated

½ tsp ground turmeric

½ tsp Easy Garam Masala (page 172)

10 to 12 grape or cherry tomatoes, cut in half lengthwise

½ medium jalapeño chili, thinly sliced (see Variations)

¼ cup (60 ml) water

To prepare the halibut, place the halibut fillets in a shallow bowl or a plate. Drizzle them with the lemon juice. Sprinkle the fillets with the turmeric, black pepper and salt, making sure each fillet is evenly covered with the seasonings. Let the fillets sit on the counter while you prepare the rest of the recipe.

To make the spiced coconut milk broth, place the inner pot in the Instant Pot and press the **Sauté** button. When the display reads "Hot," add the coconut oil. When the oil starts to shimmer, carefully add the curry leaves—take a couple of steps back from the Instant Pot as soon as you add the leaves, as they will splutter.

Let the curry leaves splutter and fry in the hot oil for 45 to 60 seconds, until the leaves curl up on the edges and turn slightly translucent. Remove them from the oil and set them aside on a layer of paper towels to drain.

Add in the mustard seeds and asafetida. When the seeds sizzle and the asafetida froths, add the onion. Season the mixture with salt to help the onion soften. Sauté the mixture for about 5 minutes, stirring it frequently, until the onion is translucent.

Add the ginger and garlic and sauté the mixture for 1 minute. Add the turmeric and Easy Garam Masala and sauté the mixture for 30 seconds to let the spices bloom.

Add the tomatoes and jalapeño slices. Stir the ingredients to combine them.

Press the **Cancel** button to turn off the Instant Pot. Pour in the water and deglaze the bottom of the pot by scraping it with a wooden spoon. This is an important step; if the bottom of the pot is not deglazed well, the "burn" error might appear during the pressure-cooking stage.

(continued)

Meen Moilee *(continued)*

1 (14-oz [420-ml]) can light coconut milk

½ medium lemon or lime, thinly sliced

4 to 5 sprigs fresh cilantro, leaves roughly chopped, for garnishing

For Serving

Steamed Sona Masuri rice or basmati rice

Appams or idiappams (see Note)

Add the coconut milk and stir to combine the ingredients. Taste the mixture and adjust the seasonings if needed.

Place the marinated fish fillets in the spiced coconut milk and add the lemon slices.

Close the Instant Pot's lid and turn the steam-release valve to the sealing position. Press the **Manual/Pressure Cook** button and set the timer for 4 minutes at **low pressure**. If you are using thinner fillets or cubed fish, decrease the cooking time to 2 minutes.

When the cooking is complete, open the lid using a quick pressure release.

Garnish the halibut with the cilantro. Serve the halibut and broth immediately, spooned over a bed of rice and appams. Top each serving with the reserved fried curry leaves.

Note:

Appams are bowl-shaped pancakes made from fermented rice batter and coconut milk. Idiappams are steamed noodle nests made from the same ingredients. Both are available in the frozen section of Indian grocery stores.

Variations

• You can substitute the fish with shrimp, prawns or scallops. Use the same settings for time and pressure.

• If you prefer a milder curry, use less jalapeño or omit it entirely.

• Make this dish vegan by using a combination of vegetables like cauliflower, carrots, peas, corn, green beans and spinach in place of fish. Cook the recipe using the **Manual/Pressure Cook** function for 3 minutes at **high pressure**, followed by a quick pressure release to depressurize the Instant Pot.

Bhapa Shorshe Maach

(Steamed Mustard Salmon)

I fell in love with the combination of salmon and mustard after trying a couple of different recipes by Food Network chef Ina Garten. While looking for inspiration to put an Indian spin on her recipes, I stumbled upon recipes for Bengali-style fish steamed in mustard sauce. I tried a bunch of different combinations for the mustard sauce and came up with a really delicious one using some classic ingredients like mustard oil, yogurt and grated coconut along with some unconventional ones like jarred stone-ground mustard and fresh dill.

The Instant Pot is a pro at steaming fish without overcooking it. Slathered with a generous amount of the awesome sauce, this salmon is steamed to perfection in just three minutes!

Serves 2

Sauce

¼ cup (25 g) grated fresh or thawed frozen coconut

2 tbsp (30 ml) stone-ground mustard

¼ cup (60 ml) plain, unsweetened Greek yogurt

1 tbsp (15 ml) mustard oil or neutral oil of choice

¼ tsp ground turmeric

¼ tsp cumin seeds

Salt, as needed

4 to 5 black peppercorns

2 tbsp (12 g) roughly chopped fresh dill

Salmon

1 lb (454 g) of 1- to 1½-inch (2.5- to 4-cm)-thick skin-on salmon steaks or fillets (see Variations)

2 to 3 green bird's-eye chilies, slit in half lengthwise but not slit through entirely, or thinly sliced jalapeño chilies

1 cup (240 ml) water

Fresh cilantro leaves, for garnishing

For Serving

Steamed basmati rice

Lime or lemon wedges (optional)

To make the sauce, combine the coconut, stone-ground mustard, Greek yogurt, mustard oil, turmeric, cumin seeds, salt, peppercorns and dill in a food grinder or mini food processor. Process the ingredients until they are smooth.

To make the salmon, set out a heatproof glass dish that fits in the Instant Pot. Alternatively, you can use an Instant Pot insert pan. Pour one-third of the sauce into the dish, spreading it to coat the bottom of the dish or the pan evenly.

Place the salmon on top of the sauce and pour the remaining two-thirds of the sauce over the fish. Spread the sauce to cover the fish evenly. Place the bird's-eye chilies on top of the salmon.

Place the inner pot in the Instant Pot and add the water to it. Place the trivet inside the pot, then place the dish or the insert pan on the trivet.

Close the Instant Pot's lid and turn the steam-release valve to the sealing position. Press the **Steam** button and adjust the timer to 3 minutes at **low pressure**. When the cooking is complete, open the lid using a quick pressure release to depressurize the Instant Pot.

Garnish the salmon with the cilantro and serve it hot with the rice and lime wedges (if using).

Variations

- You may use any type of fish you like for this recipe!
- Make it vegetarian by substituting the fish with potatoes sliced ¼ inch (6 mm) thick. Use the same time and pressure settings and, after the cooking is complete, allow the pressure to release naturally for 13 to 15 minutes.

Hearty Rice and Grains

Rice and grains are a staple in India and also in my house! On most weeknights, white or brown basmati rice or quinoa is cooked pot-in-pot in my Instant Pot to go on the side of the main dish that I'm cooking. In addition, I also use other varieties of Indian rice like Ambemohor, Ponni or Sona Masuri to serve on the side of traditional dishes. Now that I have the Instant Pot, I never make rice any other way! It comes out perfectly cooked, every single time, period.

In addition to being the essential side to almost any main dish, basmati rice is the star ingredient in fragrant rice pilafs, like the Yakhni Pulao (Rice Pilaf with Lamb in Spiced Bone Broth; page 109) or the classic biryanis like the Zafrani Chicken Biryani (Saffron Rice with Saffron Chicken; page 107) and the Kathal Biryani (Rice with Spiced Green Jackfruit; page 102). I'm also sharing the recipe for Masale Bhaat (Spiced Rice Pilaf; page 100), a very traditional Maharashtrian rice preparation that uses a local variety of rice called Ambemohor. I also love to cook brown basmati rice for dishes other than a plain side and am sharing my go-to recipe for the comforting Khichadi (Brown Basmati Rice with Brown Lentils; page 104).

Aside from rice, the most-used grains in my house are in the form of flour for making different kinds of rotis (unleavened flatbreads) like whole wheat atta, jowar (sorghum) or bajra (pearl millet). I also use sooji or rava (semolina) or daliya (bulgur wheat) to make the Upma (Bulgur Wheat Pilaf; page 114), a popular breakfast or snack food. Lastly, you'll also find a recipe for India's favorite sabudana khichadi, but with a twist—I use Israeli pearl couscous instead of tapioca pearls to make my Pearl Couscous Khichadi (Pearl Couscous Pilaf; page 113). I hope you'll love it as much as I do!

Masale Bhaat

(Spiced Rice Pilaf)

This mildly spiced rice pilaf topped with a generous drizzle of melted ghee and a nice squeeze of lime was a must at every holiday meal when I was growing up, as well at all the weddings that I attended. This dish is a classic preparation made with the Maharashtrian goda ("sweet") masala that gives the dish its characteristic warm flavor with a subtle hint of sweetness. Traditionally, it is made with a short-grain rice, Ambemohar, that is indigenous to the region, but basmati works very well too. I love it with tendli or tindora (ivy gourd, available in most Indian grocery stores, which adds a wonderful crunch). But you can skip it or use any other vegetable you like!

Serves 4

1½ cups (300 g) uncooked Ambemohar rice or basmati rice (see Note and Variations)

2 tbsp (30 ml) neutral oil of choice

½ tsp mustard seeds

½ tsp ground turmeric

¼ tsp asafetida

5 to 6 fresh curry leaves

2 cups (225 g) tendli/tindora (young ivy gourds), quartered lengthwise (see Variations)

2 tsp (4 g) Quick Goda Masala (page 175)

Salt, as needed

2 cups (480 ml) water

2 tbsp (12 g) grated fresh or thawed frozen coconut, for garnishing

8 to 10 sprigs fresh cilantro, leaves roughly chopped, for garnishing

Lime or lemon wedges, for serving

Melted ghee, for serving

Note: Ambemohar is a short-grain rice grown in the state of Maharashtra. It is available in Indian stores or online on Amazon.

Rinse the rice under cold tap water until the water turns clear. Set the rice aside.

Place the inner pot in the Instant Pot and press the **Sauté** button. When the display reads "Hot," add the oil, mustard seeds, turmeric and asafetida. When the seeds sizzle and the turmeric and asafetida froth, add the curry leaves and ivy gourd. Stir the ingredients to combine them, and sauté the mixture for 1 minute. Add the Quick Goda Masala, season the mixture with salt and mix everything together well.

Press the **Cancel** button to turn off the Instant Pot.

Add the rice and water. Stir the ingredients gently to combine them well. Taste the mixture and adjust the seasonings if needed.

Close the Instant Pot's lid and turn the steam-release valve to the sealing position. Press the **Rice** button and use the default settings for time and pressure, 12 minutes at **low pressure**. When the cooking is complete, allow the pressure to release naturally—which will take 10 to 12 minutes—and then open the lid.

Transfer the pilaf to a serving bowl or a deep platter. Garnish the pilaf with the coconut and cilantro. Serve it warm with the lime wedges and melted ghee.

Variations

• Substitute the ivy gourd with baby eggplant, pearl or sliced onions, shredded cabbage or Brussels sprouts, cauliflower florets, peas or shrimp. Use the same settings for time and pressure.

• Replace ½ cup (100 g) of the rice with ½ cup (105 g) of moong dal (split green gram) for a protein boost. Use the same water ratio and the same settings for time and pressure.

Kathal Biryani

(Rice with Spiced Green Jackfruit)

Yes, this is a biryani recipe with jackfruit as the key ingredient! While the ripe fruit is sweet, the young, green jackfruit tastes like heart of palm. When I was growing up, we had a huge jackfruit tree in our backyard. We would pluck many jackfruits while they were green for making homemade chips, pickles and the classic Maharashtrian stir-fry, fanasachi bhaji, the recipe for which is on my website.

The tropical fruit is considered a vegetarian meat substitute, with its resemblance to pulled or shredded meat when cooked. It is a perfect alternative to chicken or lamb in classic biryani recipes, turning them into vegan biryanis! The Instant Pot makes biryani easy and feasible on a weeknight.

Serves 4 to 6

Marinade

1 lb (454 g) fresh or thawed frozen young green jackfruit chunks (see Notes and Variations)

½ tsp ground turmeric

½ tsp ground cumin

½ tsp ground coriander

Red chili powder, as needed

1 tbsp (9 g) besan (chickpea flour)

Salt, as needed

Biryani

2 cups (400 g) uncooked basmati rice

¼ cup (60 ml) neutral oil of choice

2 medium onions, thinly sliced

Salt, as needed

½-inch (1.3-cm) piece fresh ginger, finely grated

2 cloves garlic, finely grated

2 tsp (4 g) biryani masala (see Notes)

1 small tomato, pureed

2 cups (480 ml) water

4 to 5 sprigs fresh cilantro, leaves roughly chopped, for garnishing

Basic Raita (page 179), for serving

To make the marinade, place the jackfruit in a medium bowl. Sprinkle the turmeric, cumin, coriander, red chili powder, chickpea flour and salt over the jackfruit. Toss the jackfruit to coat it evenly in the spices. Let the jackfruit marinate on the counter while you prepare the rest of the recipe.

To make the biryani, rinse the rice under cold tap water until the water runs clear. Set the rice aside.

Place the inner pot in the Instant Pot and press the **Sauté** button. When the display reads "Hot," add the oil and onions. Season the onions with salt to help them soften. Fry the onions for 18 to 20 minutes, stirring them frequently, until they are golden brown. Set aside about one-third of the fried onions for garnishing the dish.

Add the ginger and garlic to the pot and sauté the mixture for 1 minute. Add the biryani masala and sauté the mixture for 30 seconds to let the spices bloom.

Add the tomato and stir the ingredients to combine them. Deglaze the bottom of the pot by scraping it with a wooden spoon. This is an important step; if the bottom of the pot is not deglazed well, the "burn" error might appear during the pressure-cooking stage. Cook the mixture for another 5 minutes, until the tomato puree loses most of its moisture.

Stir in the marinated jackfruit and toss it gently to combine it with the biryani mixture, making sure the jackfruit chunks don't break apart. Sauté the mixture for about 1 minute, stirring it once or twice. Press the **Cancel** button to turn off the Instant Pot.

Spread the rinsed rice in an even layer on top of the spiced jackfruit chunks. Gently pour in the water without disturbing the layers of jackfruit and rice, ensuring the rice is fully immersed.

Close the Instant Pot's lid and turn the steam-release valve to the sealing position. Press the **Rice** button and use the default settings for time and pressure, 12 minutes at **low pressure**. When the cooking is complete, allow the pressure to release naturally—which will take 10 to 12 minutes—and then open the lid.

Transfer the biryani to a serving bowl or a deep platter. Garnish the biryani with the reserved fried onions and cilantro. Serve it warm with the Basic Raita on the side.

Notes:

• You can find fresh or frozen young green jackfruit in Indian or Asian grocery stores. Canned green jackfruit is also available at some grocery stores or online on Amazon. If you use the canned variety, rinse it well and soak it in hot water for 30 minutes to lessen the briny flavor.

• Biryani masala is readily available in Indian stores or on Amazon or other online retailers. If you cannot find it, you can substitute it with the same amount of Easy Garam Masala (page 172) with 1 dried bay leaf, 3 to 4 petals of star anise, 1 pod black cardamom and 4 to 5 black peppercorns added to it.

Variations

• Replace the jackfruit with mushrooms, artichoke hearts, paneer or shrimp. Use the same settings for time and pressure.

• You can use pieces of boneless, skinless chicken thighs or lamb in the recipe. Substitute 1 tablespoon (9 g) of chickpea flour in the marinade with 2 tablespoons (30 ml) of plain, unsweetened Greek yogurt. Sauté the meat for 4 to 5 minutes before layering on the rinsed rice. Follow the rest of the recipe's directions for cooking the rice and meat together.

*See photo on page 184.

Khichadi

(Brown Basmati Rice with Brown Lentils)

Khichadi, also known as khichri or khichdi, is the ultimate comfort food and a nutritious, Instant Pot–friendly concoction made by cooking rice and dal (lentils) together. It is my go-to meal whenever I'm under the weather or when I just need a comforting hug in a bowl.

Over the years, I have created numerous combinations of dal and rice for my khichadi recipe. I'm sharing one that is inspired by the Lebanese mujadara, masoor khichadi, made with whole masoor dal (brown lentils) and brown basmati rice cooked together with fried onions. It's delicious and comforting!

Serves 4

1 cup (192 g) whole masoor dal (brown lentils; see Variations)

1 cup (200 g) uncooked brown basmati rice

2 tbsp (30 ml) melted ghee

1 large onion, thickly sliced

Salt, as needed

1 tsp cumin seeds

4 cloves garlic, roughly chopped

½ tbsp (3 g) Easy Garam Masala (page 172)

3 cups (720 ml) water, vegetable stock or chicken stock

4 to 5 sprigs fresh cilantro, leaves roughly chopped, for garnishing

1 medium green onion, finely chopped, for garnishing

Plain, unsweetened Greek yogurt, for serving

Radishes, thickly sliced, for serving (optional)

Rinse the lentils and rice together under cold tap water. Set the mixture aside.

Place the inner pot in the Instant Pot and press the **Sauté** button. When the display reads "Hot," add the ghee and onion. Season the onion with salt to help it soften. Sauté the onion, for 8 to 10 minutes, stirring it frequently, until it is golden brown. Reserve about ¼ cup (53 g) of the fried onion for garnishing the khichadi.

Add the cumin seeds, garlic and Easy Garam Masala to the onion remaining in the pot and sauté for 1 minute. Add the rinsed rice and lentils. Season the mixture with additional salt and sauté it for 2 minutes, stirring it frequently to ensure the rice and lentils are mixed well with the seasoned onion. Add the water and stir to combine. Deglaze the pot by scraping it with a wooden spoon. This is an important step; if the bottom of the pot is not deglazed well, the "burn" error might appear during the pressure-cooking stage.

Press the **Cancel** button to turn off the Instant Pot. Close the Instant Pot's lid and turn the steam-release valve to the sealing position. Press the **Multigrain** button, and then press the **Adjust** button to set the timer for 20 minutes at **high pressure**. When the cooking is complete, allow the pressure to release naturally—which will take 15 to 20 minutes—and then open the lid.

Gently fluff the khichadi with a fork. Do not overmix, or it will become mushy.

Garnish the khichadi with the reserved fried onions, cilantro and green onion. Serve it hot with the Greek yogurt and sliced radishes (if using).

Variations

• Substitute brown lentils with the same quantity of split green gram with husk (moong chilka) or whole black gram with husk (whole urad dal).

• For a vitamin boost, mix in chopped kale or spinach along with the lentils and rice and cook everything together.

Zafrani Chicken Biryani

(Saffron Rice with Saffron Chicken)

This biryani is relatively mild in flavor and gets its gorgeous golden color from saffron, both in the marinade for the chicken and in the saffron-infused milk that is drizzled on top before serving.

Making biryani in the Instant Pot is faster and easier than the traditional stovetop method. The process is actually reversed, where the meat is cooked about halfway as an initial step, then rice is layered on top of it and both finish cooking together in the second stage. This is contrary to the stovetop method, where rice is cooked about three-fourths of the way and layered on top of marinated meat, then both are cooked together low-and-slow for over an hour.

Serves 6 to 8

Marinade

½ tsp Kashmiri saffron threads

½ cup (120 ml) warm milk

¼ cup (65 g) raw almond butter or ¼ cup (24 g) almond flour

¼ cup (60 ml) plain, unsweetened Greek yogurt

½-inch (1.3-cm) piece fresh ginger, finely grated

2 cloves garlic, finely grated

5 to 6 green bird's-eye chilies, stems removed and minced (see Variations)

1 tbsp (6 g) biryani masala (see Note)

Salt, as needed

¼ cup (24 g) roughly chopped fresh mint leaves

2 lb (908 g) bone-in, skinless chicken drumsticks and thighs (see Variations)

Biryani

¼ cup (60 ml) neutral oil of choice

3 medium onions, thinly sliced

Salt, as needed

3½ cups (840 ml) water, divided

To make the marinade, soak the Kashmiri saffron threads in the milk for about 30 minutes.

In the meantime, whisk together the almond butter, Greek yogurt, ginger, garlic, bird's-eye chilies, biryani masala, salt and mint in a large bowl.

Once the Kashmiri saffron is infused into the milk, whisk ¼ cup (60 ml) of the milk, along with a few saffron threads, into the marinade. Reserve the remaining saffron milk to top the cooked rice.

Add the chicken pieces to the marinade and toss them to ensure that they are all coated evenly. Let the chicken marinate on the counter while you prepare the rest of the recipe. Alternatively, if you have time, you can marinate the chicken in the refrigerator for 8 hours, or up to overnight. If you marinate the chicken in the refrigerator, let the chicken sit out at room temperature for 30 to 60 minutes before cooking it.

To make the biryani, place the inner pot in the Instant Pot and press the **Sauté** button. When the display reads "Hot," add the oil and onions. Season the onions with salt to help them soften. Fry the onions for 18 to 20 minutes, stirring them frequently, until they are golden brown.

Press the **Cancel** button to turn off the Instant Pot.

Reserve about one-third of the fried onions for garnishing the dish.

Add ½ cup (120 ml) of the water to the pot. Deglaze the bottom of the pot by scraping it with a wooden spoon. This is an important step; if the bottom of the pot is not deglazed well, the "burn" error might appear during the pressure-cooking stage.

Stir in the marinated chicken and toss the chicken with the fried onions to combine everything well.

(continued)

Zafrani Chicken Biryani *(continued)*

3 cups (600 g) basmati rice

1 tbsp (14 g) ghee

4 to 5 sprigs fresh mint, leaves roughly chopped, for garnishing

4 to 5 sprigs fresh cilantro, leaves roughly chopped, for garnishing

For Serving

Basic Raita (page 179)

Note:

Biryani masala is readily available in Indian stores or on Amazon or other online retailers. If you cannot find it, you can substitute it with the same amount of Easy Garam Masala (page 172), with 1 dried bay leaf, 3 to 4 petals of star anise, 1 pod of black cardamom and 4 to 5 black peppercorns added.

Close the Instant Pot's lid and turn the steam-release valve to the sealing position. Press the **Poultry** or **Manual/Pressure Cook** button and set the timer for 5 minutes at **high pressure**. When the cooking is complete, open the lid using a quick pressure release to depressurize the Instant Pot.

Press the **Cancel** button to turn off the Instant Pot. Stir the cooked chicken and scrape the bottom of the pot if needed.

Rinse the rice under cold tap water and spread it in an even layer on top of the partially cooked chicken. Dot the top of the rice with the ghee.

Dissolve the desired amount of salt in the remaining 3 cups (720 ml) of water. Gently pour the salted water over the rice without disturbing the layers of chicken and rice, ensuring that the rice is fully immersed. Gently stick the blunt end of a wooden spoon in 4 quadrants of the pot to make sure the water seeps all the way down to the bottom of the pot.

Close the Instant Pot's lid and turn the steam-release valve to the sealing position. Press the **Rice** button and use the default settings for time and pressure, 12 minutes at **low pressure**. When the cooking is complete, allow the pressure to release naturally—which will take 15 to 20 minutes—and then open the lid.

Transfer the biryani to a serving bowl or a deep platter and drizzle it with the remaining saffron milk. Garnish it with the reserved fried onions, mint and cilantro. Serve the biryani warm with the Basic Raita on the side.

Variations

• If you prefer a milder flavor, use serrano or jalapeño chilies instead of bird's-eye chilies.

• Substitute the chicken with bone-in lamb or goat meat. Increase the meat's cooking time to 25 minutes.

• Make this biryani vegetarian by substituting chicken with paneer. Marinate the paneer as you would the chicken, but skip the cooking process detailed in the recipe, as paneer doesn't need to be cooked. Simply toss the marinated paneer with the fried onions and then layer the rinsed rice on top of the onions and paneer. Follow the rest of the directions for cooking the rice and paneer together.

Yakhni Pulao

(Rice Pilaf with Lamb in Spiced Bone Broth)

Yakhni pulao, a specialty of Kashmir, is a hearty rice pilaf made by cooking rice in yakhni, which is spiced bone broth. The Instant Pot's Soup/Broth function comes in handy for making the most flavorful yakhni—and in half the time. While this dish is primarily made with goat or lamb, you can find variations with chicken or beef and also vegetarian versions.

The traditional recipes for yakhni pulao with meat do not call for the addition of vegetables, but I love to turn the volume up on my pulao and serve it studded with peas and baby potatoes! I think it makes for a balanced rice dish that can stand on its own as a main.

Serves 6 to 8

Yakhni

2 lb (908 g) bone-in lamb stew meat (see Variation)

3 cups (720 ml) water

1 small onion, unpeeled and quartered

1-inch (2.5-cm) piece fresh ginger, unpeeled and quartered

5 to 6 cloves garlic, unpeeled

1 tbsp (6 g) fennel seeds

3 tbsp (18 g) coriander seeds

2 dried bay leaves

2 to 3 (1-inch [2.5-cm]) pieces cinnamon bark

1 tsp black peppercorns

2 pods black cardamom

5 to 6 pods green cardamom

8 to 10 whole cloves

2 star anise

Salt, as needed

To make the yakhni, place the lamb, water, onion, ginger, garlic, fennel seeds, coriander seeds, bay leaves, cinnamon bark pieces, peppercorns, black cardamom, green cardamom, cloves, star anise and salt in the inner pot of the Instant Pot. Gently stir the ingredients to combine them, and then place the inner pot in the Instant Pot.

Close the Instant Pot's lid and turn the steam-release valve to the sealing position. Press the **Soup/Broth** button and set the timer for 25 minutes at **high pressure**. When the cooking is complete, allow the pressure to release naturally—which will take 18 to 20 minutes—and then open the lid.

Using a pair of tongs, carefully remove the cooked lamb and transfer it to a medium bowl. Set the bowl aside. Strain the spiced broth into a large bowl or measuring cup and set it aside.

To make the pulao, rinse the rice under cold tap water. Set the rice aside.

Variation

Substitute the lamb with bone-in chicken drumsticks and thighs, and decrease the cooking time for the yakhni to 10 minutes.

(continued)

Yakhni Pulao *(continued)*

Pulao

3 cups (600 g) uncooked basmati rice

2 tbsp (30 ml) neutral oil of choice

1 large onion, thinly sliced

Salt, as needed

½ tsp cumin seeds

½-inch (1.3-cm) piece fresh ginger, finely grated

2 cloves garlic, finely grated

2 to 3 green bird's-eye chilies, halved lengthwise

4 to 5 baby potatoes, halved

½ cup (67 g) fresh or frozen peas

2 tbsp (30 ml) plain, unsweetened Greek yogurt

4 to 5 sprigs fresh cilantro, leaves roughly chopped, for garnishing (optional)

For Serving

Basic Raita (page 179)

Place the inner pot back in the Instant Pot. If you want, you can wipe it with a damp paper towel, but it is not necessary to do so.

Press the **Sauté** button. When the display reads "Hot," add the oil and onion. Season the onion with salt to help it soften. Sauté the onion for 8 to 10 minutes, stirring it frequently, until it is golden brown. Reserve about ¼ cup (53 g) of the fried onions for garnishing the pulao.

Add the cumin seeds, ginger and garlic to the onion remaining in the pot. Sauté the mixture for 1 minute, until the mixture no longer smells raw. Add the bird's-eye chilies, potatoes, peas and Greek yogurt. Stir the ingredients well to combine them.

Press the **Cancel** button to turn off the Instant Pot. Add the cooked lamb and the rinsed rice. Pour in the spiced broth and stir to combine everything. Taste the mixture and add more salt if needed.

Close the Instant Pot's lid and turn the steam-release valve to the sealing position. Press the **Rice** button and use the default settings for time and pressure, 12 minutes at **low pressure**. When the cooking is complete, allow the pressure to release naturally—which will take 10 to 12 minutes—and then open the lid.

Transfer the pulao to a serving bowl or a deep platter. Garnish it with the reserved fried onions and cilantro (if using). Serve the pulao warm with the Basic Raita on the side.

Pearl Couscous Khichadi

(Pearl Couscous Pilaf)

Sabudana khichadi ("tapioca pearls pilaf") is extremely popular among Indians and is usually made for religious fasting, but it is also good for a light lunch, a hearty breakfast or an afternoon snack. It is my mom's signature concoction, and you can find a detailed recipe for it on my website.

While I have perfected my mom's recipe over the years, it does take a bit of time to prepare the tapioca pearls before they can be used. So I came up with a hack and re-created the classic flavors using a new key ingredient, Israeli pearl couscous, and a new technique for making it, the Instant Pot. Give it a try!

Serves 2 to 4

2 tbsp (28 g) ghee or 2 tbsp (30 ml) neutral oil of choice

1 tsp cumin seeds

1 green bird's-eye chili, thinly sliced (optional)

1 cup (150 g) quartered baby potatoes

Salt, as needed

½ tsp sugar

1 cup (135 g) uncooked Israeli pearl couscous (see Variations)

1½ cups (360 ml) water

Juice of ½ medium lime

⅓ cup (40 g) crushed unsalted roasted peanuts

¼ cup (25 g) grated fresh or thawed frozen coconut, divided

18 to 20 sprigs fresh cilantro, leaves roughly chopped, divided

Lime or lemon wedges, for serving

Place the inner pot in the Instant Pot and press the **Sauté** button. When the display reads "Hot," add the ghee and allow it to melt. Add the cumin seeds and bird's-eye chili (if using). Let the seeds and chili sizzle for about 30 seconds, and then add the potatoes.

Season the potatoes with the salt and sugar and mix everything together well. Add the couscous and stir the ingredients to combine them. Sauté the mixture for 1 minute, allowing the couscous to become coated with the ghee and seasonings and become lightly toasted. Press the **Cancel** button.

Pour in the water and stir the ingredients well. Deglaze the bottom of the pot by scraping it with a wooden spoon. This is an important step; if the bottom of the pot is not deglazed well, the "burn" error might appear during the pressure-cooking stage. Add the lime juice and stir to combine.

Close the Instant Pot's lid and turn the steam-release valve to the sealing position. Press the **Manual/Pressure Cook** button and set the timer for 5 minutes at **high pressure**. When cooking is complete, allow the pressure to release naturally—which will take 12 to 15 minutes—and then open the lid. Press the **Cancel** button.

Using a fork, gently fluff the couscous, making sure the potatoes don't break apart or get mashed. Add the peanuts and stir gently to combine.

Gently stir in the coconut and cilantro, reserving 1 tablespoon (6 g) of coconut and 1 tablespoon (1 g) of the cilantro for garnishing. Sprinkle the reserved coconut and cilantro on top of the khichadi and serve it immediately with the lime wedges.

Variations
• Substitute the Israeli pearl couscous with quinoa and follow the recipe as it is written.

• Toss in diced cucumbers just before serving the khichadi for a cool, refreshing crunch.

Upma

(Bulgur Wheat Pilaf)

Upma is a classic, savory porridge made with vegetables and rava or sooji, which is essentially farina, as the key ingredient. It's a hearty, comforting dish that is popular for breakfast or an afternoon snack in India. While I often make the original version, every once in a while, I like to switch it up with bulgur wheat (wheat daliya, as it's called in India) as the key ingredient, along with cannellini beans. It's a recipe inspired by the Lebanese chickpea and bulgur pilaf.

I like to use the Instant Pot's Rice function for this recipe. The bulgur wheat comes out perfectly cooked and fluffy every single time!

Serves 3 to 4

2 tbsp (30 ml) neutral oil of choice

1 tsp cumin seeds

5 to 6 fresh curry leaves

1 to 2 dried round red chilies or 1 dried long red chili

1 small onion, roughly chopped

Salt, as needed

4 to 5 cloves garlic, roughly chopped

2 medium tomatoes, diced

1 cup (165 g) uncooked bulgur wheat (see Variations)

2 cups (480 ml) water, vegetable stock or chicken stock

4 leaves kale, stems trimmed and roughly chopped (see Variations)

4 to 5 sprigs fresh cilantro, leaves roughly chopped, for garnishing

1 medium green onion, thinly sliced, for garnishing

Place the inner pot in the Instant Pot and press the **Sauté** button. When the display reads "Hot," add the oil, cumin seeds, curry leaves and round red chilies. When the seeds sizzle and the curry leaves splutter, add the onion. Season the onion with salt to help it soften. Sauté the mixture for 5 to 7 minutes, stirring it frequently, until the onion is translucent.

Stir in the garlic and sauté the mixture for 1 minute. Add the tomatoes and deglaze the bottom of the pot by scraping it with a wooden spoon.

Sauté the mixture for 4 to 5 minutes, until the tomatoes soften and lose some of their moisture. Add the bulgur wheat. Season the mixture with additional salt and combine the ingredients well. Press the **Cancel** button to turn off the Instant Pot. Pour in the water and add the kale. Stir the ingredients gently to combine them well.

Close the Instant Pot's lid and turn the steam-release valve to the sealing position. Press the **Rice** button and use the default settings for time and pressure, 12 minutes at **low pressure**. When the cooking is complete, open the lid using a quick pressure release to depressurize the Instant Pot.

Fluff the upma with a fork and garnish it with the cilantro and green onion. Serve it warm or at room temperature.

Variations

• Use quinoa in place of bulgur wheat. Use 1½ cups (360 ml) of water for 1 cup (170 g) of quinoa. Use the same settings for time and pressure, but depressurize the Instant Pot using a natural pressure release, which will take 8 to 10 minutes.

• You can substitute the kale with any other leafy green, like baby spinach or arugula. Add the greens after cooking is complete and let the leaves wilt for 8 to 10 minutes before serving the upma.

• Mix in shredded rotisserie chicken or cubes of grilled chicken breast for a protein boost.

Bites and *Small* Plates

I love hosting and entertaining, but most of all I love to party! Be it with family on a Friday night or with friends on weekends or festive occasions, when I throw a soiree, delectable party food is certainly at the front and center of the evening.

The recipes in this chapter include street-food bites like Anda Chaat (Street Food–Style Deviled Eggs; page 118) and Ragda Puri (White Pea Curry in Crisp Dough Balls; page 123) that you can serve at "chaat parties"; finger foods like Drums of Heaven (Chicken Wings; page 127), which will be a winner at your game-day party; and small plates that are perfect for easy entertaining, like Pulled Pork Vindaloo Tacos (page 133), to which guests can help themselves at the taco bar, or Patra Ni Machhi (Steamed Fish in Banana Leaves; page 130), the elegant fish packets that will wow your guests at the dinner table!

Kanchipuram Idlis (Turmeric-Spiced Rice and Lentil Cakes; page 124) are perfect bites to kick off a traditional South Indian weekend brunch on holidays or festive occasions. And Kheema Pav (Sloppy Joes; page 134) is great for a laid-back movie night.

The Instant Pot makes entertaining with homemade food very easy—go have fun with the guests at your party instead of slaving in the kitchen by yourself!

Anda Chaat

(Street Food–Style Deviled Eggs)

I'm a huge lover of chaat, the Indian street food. With its sweet, sour, spicy and savory combination of flavors, each bite of chaat is a mouthful of heaven! Anda chaat, or egg chaat, is the idea behind this recipe that I created to Indianize deviled eggs. I love it because it combines the amazing flavors of chaat with one of the most nutritious foods on earth.

The Instant Pot is great for making hard-boiled eggs in this recipe. You don't have to babysit the eggs. Just set them to pressure-cook for five minutes, and they will come out perfectly every single time!

Serves 8

1 cup (240 ml) water

8 large eggs

½ cup (120 ml) plain, unsweetened Greek yogurt or sour cream

1 tsp ground cumin

1 tsp ground coriander

Salt, as needed

Kashmiri red chili powder, for garnishing

Tamarind-date chutney, for garnishing

½ small red onion, thinly sliced, for garnishing

½ small tomato, seeded and finely chopped, for garnishing

4 to 5 sprigs fresh cilantro, leaves roughly chopped, for garnishing

Sev, for garnishing

Add the water to the inner pot of the Instant Pot. Place the metal trivet in the pot. Gently place the eggs on top of the trivet.

Close the Instant Pot's lid and turn the steam-release valve to the sealing position. Press the **Egg** or **Manual/Pressure Cook** button and set the timer for 5 minutes at **high pressure**. When the cooking is complete, open the lid using a quick pressure release to depressurize the Instant Pot.

Transfer the eggs to a medium bowl of cold tap water and allow them to cool for 5 minutes. Drain the water, then crack and peel the eggs carefully. Gently dry them with a paper towel. Slice the eggs in half lengthwise and scoop the cooked yolks into a small bowl, but place the whites on a serving platter.

Mash the yolks into a fine crumble using a fork. Add the Greek yogurt, cumin, coriander and salt and mix everything together well. Fill the inside of the egg white with the yolk mixture using a spoon, mini ice cream scoop or piping bag fitted with a decorative tip.

Sprinkle each deviled egg with a pinch of the Kashmiri red chili powder and drizzle a few drops of the tamarind-date chutney on top. Garnish the eggs with the red onion, tomato, cilantro and sev. Serve the eggs immediately.

Ragda Puri

(White Pea Curry in Crisp Dough Balls)

Ragda puri is a popular Maharashtrian street food that originated in Mumbai Chowpatty, a public beach in Mumbai famous for its street-food joints. Hot, bubbly and mildly spiced, curried white peas (i.e., ragda) are stuffed in crunchy, deep-fried dough balls (i.e., puris) along with cubes of boiled potato and topped with red onion, tomato, cilantro, lip-smacking tamarind-date chutney and some crispy sev.

With the Instant Pot, making the pea curry is a breeze. You can cook the dried peas without soaking them and instantly satisfy your Chowpatty food cravings!

Serves 6 to 8

Ragda

2 tbsp (30 ml) neutral oil of choice

½ tsp cumin seeds

½ tsp mustard seeds

¼ tsp asafetida

1 medium onion, finely chopped

Salt, as needed

½ tsp ground turmeric

½ tsp ground cumin

½ tsp ground coriander

Kashmiri red chili powder, as needed

1 tsp powdered jaggery or coconut palm sugar

1 medium Yukon gold potato, diced

1 cup (190 g) dried white peas or dried green peas

2½ cups (600 ml) water

For Serving

7 oz (196 g) crispy fried pani puri golgappas

Ground cumin

Kashmiri red chili powder or other Indian red chili powder

Tamarind-date chutney

½ small red onion, finely chopped

½ small tomato, seeded and finely diced

4 to 5 sprigs fresh cilantro, leaves roughly chopped

Sev

To make the ragda, place the inner pot in the Instant Pot and press the **Sauté** button. When the display reads "Hot," add the oil, cumin seeds, mustard seeds and asafetida. When the seeds sizzle and the asafetida froths, add the onion. Season the mixture with salt to help the onion soften. Sauté the mixture for 5 to 7 minutes, stirring it frequently, until the onion is translucent. Press the **Cancel** button to turn off the Instant Pot.

Season the mixture with the turmeric, ground cumin, coriander, Kashmiri red chili powder, salt and jaggery and stir to combine the ingredients well, letting the mixture cook over the residual heat while you do so. Add the potato, white peas and water. Stir the mixture to combine everything well.

Close the Instant Pot's lid and turn the steam-release valve to the sealing position. Press the **Bean/Chili** button and set the timer for 40 minutes at **high pressure**. When the cooking is complete, allow the pressure to release naturally—which will take 15 to 20 minutes—and then open the lid. Note that older dried peas may take longer to cook. If you find that your peas are not soft and haven't cooked all the way through, close the lid immediately and set the Instant Pot to **high pressure** on the **Bean/Chili** mode for another 10 minutes. Allow the pressure to release naturally. Transfer the ragda to a serving bowl.

To serve the dish, crack open a hole on top of each puri. Place 6 to 7 puris on each individual serving plate. Fill each puri's cavity with the ragda, ensuring that some of the ragda overflows out of each puri.

Sprinkle each puri with a pinch of ground cumin and a pinch of Kashmiri red chili powder. Drizzle a few drops of tamarind-date chutney on top and garnish the puris with the red onion, tomato and cilantro. Sprinkle some sev over the puris and serve them immediately.

Note: Pani puris, tamarind-date chutney, dried white peas and sev (crispy fried chickpea batter noodles, also known as bhujia) are all readily available at Indian stores. Sev comes in various sizes. I recommend the smallest and the finest or thinnest size for this recipe.

Kanchipuram Idlis

(Turmeric-Spiced Rice and Lentil Cakes)

Since I am married to a South Indian, idlis (steamed fermented rice and lentil cakes) are a regular in my house. Living close to San Francisco, I used to buy the batter at Indian stores because there are only a handful of days in the year when it gets warm enough to ferment the batter naturally. With the Instant Pot's Yogurt function, I can ferment the batter overnight, and then I can use the Steam function for steaming the cakes the next day.

When I make a batch of batter, I use half to make plain idlis and the other half to make Kanchipuram idlis by adding spices and vegetables. They taste great on their own but are amazing with Tomato Pachadi (Curry Leaf–Scented Chunky Tomato Sauce; page 165).

Makes 20 to 24 idlis

Batter

½ cup (110 g) urad gota dal (black gram without husks)

2 cups (480 ml) water, divided, plus more if needed

1 cup (190 g) idli rava (cream of rice)

Salt, as needed

Note:

If you don't plan to make the idlis right after salting the batter, you can store it in an airtight container in the refrigerator for up to 72 hours. Let the batter sit on the counter for 1 to 2 hours before using it.

To make the batter, rinse the black gram under cold tap water, and then soak it in a small bowl with 1 cup (240 ml) of the water for 4 hours. In a medium bowl, whisk together the remaining 1 cup (240 ml) of water and the idli rava, making sure it's well incorporated. Let this mixture rest alongside the black gram for 4 hours.

Once the black gram is soaked, transfer it and the soaking water to a high-powered blender or food grinder. Blend the black gram until it forms a smooth paste. Transfer the paste to the soaked idli rava and stir well to combine the two. If the batter is too thick, you can add ¼ to ½ cup (60 to 120 ml) of water to loosen it up, but make sure it's still thick, similar to easily flowing pancake batter.

Transfer the mixed batter to the inner pot and place it in the Instant Pot. Close the Instant Pot's lid. It doesn't matter whether you turn the pressure-release valve to the venting or sealing position.

Press the **Yogurt** button. Set the timer for 12 hours. After 12 hours, you will hear a beep and the Instant Pot will display "yogt." Open the lid and check to see if the batter has risen. It should have almost doubled in volume and smell a little sour. If it's not fermented, you can leave it on the **Yogurt** setting for an additional 1 to 2 hours.

To season the batter, stir in the salt and mix the fermented batter well to deflate it. Transfer it to another container and clean the inner pot so it can be used for steaming the idlis.

At this stage, the batter can be used for making plain idlis (see Note).

(continued)

Kanchipuram Idlis *(continued)*

Kanchipuram Idlis

¼ cup (34 g) thawed frozen peas or blanched fresh peas (see Variations)

¼ cup (28 g) shredded carrots (see Variations)

9 to 10 sprigs fresh cilantro, leaves roughly chopped

2 tbsp (30 ml) neutral oil of choice

½-inch (1.3-cm) piece fresh ginger, finely grated

1 green bird's-eye chili, minced (optional)

4 to 5 fresh curry leaves, roughly chopped

1 tsp urad dal (split black gram without husks)

2 tsp (12 g) roasted dalia split (roasted split chickpeas)

½ tsp mustard seeds

½ tsp cumin seeds

½ tsp freshly ground black pepper

½ tsp ground turmeric

For Steaming

Water, as needed

Neutral oil of choice or ghee, as needed

For Serving

Tomato Pachadi (page 165)

For making the Kanchipuram idlis, stir the peas, carrots and cilantro into the salted batter.

Heat the oil in a small skillet over medium heat. When the oil is shimmering, add the ginger, bird's-eye chili (if using), curry leaves, split black gram, split chickpeas, mustard seeds, cumin seeds, black pepper and turmeric. Reduce the heat to low and sauté the mixture for 3 to 4 minutes, stirring it frequently, until it no longer smells raw. Pour the mixture into the idli batter and mix everything together well.

To steam the idlis, place the inner pot in the Instant Pot and add 1 cup (240 ml) of water to it.

Grease the idli molds with the oil and add about ¼ cup (60 ml) of the prepared batter to each mold. Assemble the idli stand with the batter in the molds and place it in the inner pot.

Close the Instant Pot's lid and turn the steam-release valve to the venting position. Press the **Steam** button and set the timer for 15 minutes at **high pressure**. Set a kitchen timer for the same amount of time, because with the steam-release valve in the venting position, the Instant Pot timer does not work accurately as the pressure doesn't build up in the process.

After the steaming is complete, press the **Cancel** button. Allow the pressure to release naturally—which will take 1 to 2 minutes—and then open the lid after the pressure valve has dropped.

Open the lid and, using kitchen mitts, carefully take the idli stand out of the inner pot and let it sit, undisturbed, for 2 minutes before scraping the idlis off the molds.

Serve the idlis hot with the Tomato Pachadi.

Variations

• Add riced cauliflower and/or thinly sliced green beans to the peas and carrots to turn the volume up and lighten the batter.

• Substitute the peas and carrots with pureed spinach.

• Omit all of the ingredients for the Kanchipuram idlis and mix in grated or finely chopped broccoli or cauliflower and some shredded Cheddar cheese to the plain idli batter for a cheesy variation.

Drums of Heaven

(Chicken Wings)

Indian-Chinese cuisine includes a fantastic appetizer called drums of heaven, which are essentially deep-fried chicken wings tossed in a sweet, spicy and tangy sauce. This was a must-have every time my husband and I went to Nanking restaurant when we lived in New Jersey. After moving to the Bay Area and not finding drums of heaven on any of the restaurant menus, I developed my own recipe for it.

My recipe is healthier, as I cook the wings together with the marinade in the Instant Pot and make the wings crispy and golden brown under the broiler. The marinade is cooked and turned into a lip-smacking sauce in which the crispy wings can either be tossed or dipped.

Serves 6

Chicken Wings

4 lb (1.8 kg) chicken wings

¾ cup (96 g) Szechuan Chutney (page 168)

¾ cup (180 ml) dark soy sauce

¼ cup (60 ml) water

¾ tsp finely ground black pepper

1 tbsp (15 g) sugar

1 tbsp (15 ml) distilled white vinegar

3 to 4 green bird's-eye chilies, minced (see Note)

3 to 4 medium green onions, thickly sliced

Sauce

3 tbsp (24 g) cornstarch

3 tbsp (45 ml) water

4 to 5 sprigs fresh cilantro, leaves roughly chopped, for garnishing

1 to 2 medium green onions, thinly sliced, for garnishing

To prepare the chicken wings, place the chicken wings in the inner pot of the Instant Pot. Add the Szechuan Chutney, dark soy sauce, water, black pepper, sugar, vinegar, bird's-eye chilies and green onions. Toss the chicken wings with the marinade ingredients, ensuring all the wings are evenly coated. Allow the wings to marinate at room temperature for 20 to 30 minutes.

To cook the wings, transfer the inner pot to the Instant Pot.

Close the Instant Pot's lid and turn the steam-release valve to the sealing position. Press the **Poultry** or **Manual/Pressure Cook** button and set the timer for 8 minutes at **high pressure**. When the cooking is complete, let the pressure release naturally for 10 minutes and then open the lid using a quick pressure release to depressurize the Instant Pot.

Meanwhile, line a large baking sheet with nonstick aluminum foil, or grease it generously with cooking oil.

Using a pair of tongs, transfer the chicken wings to the prepared baking sheet. Set the baking sheet aside.

To make the sauce, whisk together the cornstarch and water in a small bowl to make a slurry. Pour the slurry into the cooked marinade that is left behind in the inner pot.

With the inner pot in the Instant Pot, press the **Sauté** button and bring the sauce to a boil, stirring it frequently. This should take 2 to 3 minutes.

Press the **Cancel** button and let the sauce continue to thicken over the Instant Pot's residual heat.

(continued)

Drums of Heaven *(continued)*

Note:
If you prefer a milder dish, use fewer bird's-eye chilies or use milder chilies, like jalapeños.

Preheat the broiler.

While the broiler preheats, use a brush to baste the wings with the sauce from the inner pot.

Broil the chicken wings for 2 to 3 minutes, until they are lightly charred.

Take the baking sheet out of the oven, flip the wings over and baste them with the sauce. Broil the wings for 2 to 3 minutes on the other side, until they are lightly charred.

Transfer the wings to a serving platter. Garnish them with the cilantro and green onions. Serve the wings immediately with the extra sauce on the side for dipping. Alternatively, you can transfer the broiled wings to the inner pot and toss them with the sauce before serving them, garnished with the cilantro and green onions.

Patra Ni Machhi

(Steamed Fish in Banana Leaves)

Patra ni machhi is a very popular Parsi dish in which fish is smeared with a generous amount of green chutney and steamed in banana-leaf packets. It can be whipped up in just a few minutes and is great for a first course but also works as a hearty meal when served along with some hot rotis or steamed rice. The green chutney packs a flavorful punch with the coconut, herbs, garlic, cumin and a hint of heat from the green chilies. The banana leaves make for a dramatic presentation and impart a wonderful flavor to the fish.

Serves 4

Green Chutney

1 cup (16 g) tightly packed fresh cilantro leaves and tender stems

¼ cup (23 g) fresh mint leaves

4 to 5 green bird's-eye chilies, roughly chopped

1-inch (2.5-cm) piece fresh ginger, roughly chopped

4 cloves garlic, smashed and peeled

1 cup (100 g) grated fresh or thawed frozen coconut

½ tsp cumin

1 tsp salt, or as needed

½ tsp sugar

Juice of ½ medium lemon

2 tbsp (30 ml) water

Steamed Fish

4 banana leaves, cut into 12 x 12–inch (30 x 30–cm) squares (see Note)

4 (4-oz [112-g], ¾-inch [2-cm]-thick) skinless sea bass fillets or fish fillets of your choice

½ medium lemon, thinly sliced, for topping (optional)

1 cup (240 ml) water

Fresh cilantro leaves, for garnishing

For Serving

1 small red onion, thickly sliced

Start by making the green chutney. In a high-powered food grinder or blender, combine the cilantro, mint, bird's-eye chilies, ginger, garlic, coconut, cumin, salt, sugar, lemon juice and water. Process the ingredients until they form a fine, smooth paste. Set the green chutney aside.

Next, begin preparing the steamed fish. Wipe the banana leaves clean with a paper towel. Microwave each leaf, one at a time, for 20 to 30 seconds on high to make it soft and pliable.

Place the prepared banana leaves on a flat surface. Smear about 1 tablespoon (8 g) of the green chutney in the center of each of the leaves. Place a sea bass fillet on top of the smeared chutney on each of the leaves. Slather the 4 fillets with the remaining green chutney. Place a lemon slice (if using) on top of each of the chutney-covered fish fillets.

Fold one side of the banana leaf over the fish, then fold the opposite side of the leaf over the first folded side. Then fold the remaining sides under to secure the packet. You can also use a toothpick to secure the two loose ends if needed.

Once the packets are ready, it's time to steam them. Place the inner pot in the Instant Pot and add the water. Place the trivet inside the pot, then insert a steamer basket, if you have one. Transfer the packets to the steamer basket or place them directly on top of the trivet.

Close the Instant Pot's lid and turn the steam-release valve to the sealing position. Press the **Steam** button and adjust the timer to 3 minutes at **low pressure**. When the cooking is complete, open the lid using a quick pressure release.

Transfer each fish packet to a plate. Open the packets and gently tuck the loose ends of the leaves under the fish. Garnish with the cilantro and serve with the red onion.

Note: If you can't find banana leaves, you can use parchment paper to make the packets.

Pulled Pork Vindaloo Tacos

My first time tasting a vindaloo curry was, surprisingly, in the United Kingdom, and I loved the tangy, spicy flavors. Years later, I tried authentic vindaloo in Goa and learned that it's actually a fusion of Portuguese and Indian food. I prefer to use the Slow Cook function of the Instant Pot for this recipe, but you can also pressure-cook it to have it ready in less than an hour.

Makes 24 mini tacos

Vindaloo Masala

15 whole dried Kashmiri red chilies, stems removed

5 whole dried spicy red chilies, stems removed (see Variations)

1-inch (2.5-cm) piece cinnamon bark

5 to 6 whole cloves

1 tsp cumin seeds

10 to 12 black peppercorns

¼ tsp mustard seeds

½ tsp ground turmeric

6 cloves garlic, peeled and smashed

1-inch (2.5-cm) piece fresh ginger, roughly chopped

¼ cup (60 ml) red wine vinegar

¼ cup (60 ml) water

Salt, as needed

Pulled Pork

2 lb (908 g) boneless pork shoulder or Boston butt roast, cut into 4 to 6 large pieces (see Variations)

2 tbsp (30 ml) neutral oil of choice

1 large onion, thinly sliced

Salt, as needed

For Serving

24 street taco–style tortillas

Shredded cabbage

1 small onion, thinly sliced

Thinly sliced radishes (optional)

2 medium jalapeño chilies, thinly sliced (optional)

Cilantro leaves

Lime wedges

To make the vindaloo masala, combine the Kashmiri red chilies, spicy red chilies, cinnamon bark, cloves, cumin seeds, peppercorns, mustard seeds, turmeric, garlic, ginger, vinegar, water and salt in a high-powered blender or food grinder. Blend the ingredients until they form a fine, smooth paste.

To make the pulled pork, place the pork shoulder in a large bowl. Pour the vindaloo masala over the pork and ensure it is evenly coated. Let the pork marinate on the counter while you prepare the rest of the recipe.

Place the inner pot in the Instant Pot and press the **Sauté** button. When the display reads "Hot," add the oil and onion. Season the onion with salt to help it soften. Sauté for about 5 minutes, until it is translucent. Press the **Cancel** button. Transfer the pork and excess vindaloo masala to the inner pot.

Close the Instant Pot's lid. The pressure-release valve can be in the venting or the sealing position. Press the **Slow Cook** button. Press the **Adjust** button to select the **More** setting and leave the time setting at the default 4 hours. After the slow-cooking is complete, press the **Cancel** button and open the lid. Alternatively, you can speed up the process by pressure-cooking the pork using the **Meat/Stew** function, set for 40 minutes at **high pressure**. When the cooking is complete, allow the pressure to release naturally—which will take 18 to 20 minutes—and then open the lid.

Gently transfer the pork to a medium bowl. Pour the vindaloo sauce in the bottom of the inner pot into a small serving bowl. Using two forks, shred the cooked pork. Pour in some of the vindaloo sauce, if the meat looks dry.

To serve the tacos, place some of the pork in the center of the tortillas and drizzle the vindaloo sauce over the meat. Top with the cabbage, onion, radishes (if using), jalapeños (if using) and cilantro. Serve the tacos with the lime wedges on the side.

Variations

- You can substitute the pork with boneless, skinless chicken thighs or boneless lamb shoulder.

- You can substitute the spicy red chilies with additional dried Kashmiri red chilies for a milder flavor.

- Serve the pork on slider buns to create Pulled Pork Vindaloo Sliders.

Kheema Pav

(Sloppy Joes)

Kheema is essentially minced meat cooked in a spicy onion-tomato masala, and pav is a slider-like soft bun, the ultimate vehicle to absorb the delicious meaty masala and mop it off the plate. Typically made with ground goat meat or chicken, it's a classic dish on the menus of humble Indian cafes and street-food joints. I love this Instant Pot–friendly recipe that is effortless and ready in no time. I like to use lean, dark-meat turkey to go with the buttery bread buns, but you can use your favorite ground meat.

Serves 4 to 6

Kheema

2 tbsp (30 ml) neutral oil of choice

1 tsp cumin seeds

¼ tsp asafetida

1 large onion, minced

Salt, as needed

½-inch (1.3-cm) piece ginger, finely grated

2 cloves garlic, finely grated

½ tsp ground turmeric

½ tsp ground cumin

½ tsp ground coriander

2 tsp (4 g) Easy Garam Masala (page 172)

1½ tsp (3 g) Kashmiri red chili powder

3 medium tomatoes, pureed

1½ lb (681 g) ground turkey thigh meat (see Variations)

¾ cup (101 g) frozen peas or fresh English peas

4 to 5 sprigs fresh cilantro, leaves roughly chopped, for garnishing

For Serving

12 Indian pav or slider buns, slit in half and lightly toasted on a flat pan with butter if desired

1 small onion, thinly sliced

1 medium jalapeño chili, thinly sliced (optional)

Lime wedges

To make the kheema, place the inner pot in the Instant Pot and press the **Sauté** button. When the display reads "Hot," add the oil, cumin seeds and asafetida. When the seeds sizzle and the asafetida froths, add the onion. Season the mixture with salt to help the onion soften. Sauté the mixture for 8 to 10 minutes, stirring it frequently, until the onion is golden brown.

Stir in the ginger and garlic and sauté the mixture for 1 minute. Add the turmeric, ground cumin, coriander, Easy Garam Masala and Kashmiri red chili powder and sauté the mixture for 30 seconds to let the spices bloom.

Mix in the pureed tomatoes and stir to combine the ingredients. Deglaze the bottom of the pot by scraping it with a wooden spoon. This is an important step; if the bottom of the pot is not deglazed well, the "burn" error might appear during the pressure-cooking stage. Cook the mixture for 5 minutes, until the tomatoes have lost most of their moisture. Press the **Cancel** button.

Add the turkey and the peas and stir to combine the ingredients well. Close the Instant Pot's lid and turn the steam-release valve to the sealing position. Press the **Poultry** or **Manual/Pressure Cook** button and set the timer for 10 minutes at **high pressure**. When the cooking is complete, allow the pressure to release naturally—which will take 15 to 20 minutes—and then open the lid.

Press the **Sauté** button and simmer the kheema for 3 to 5 minutes, stirring it occasionally, to evaporate the extra liquid that the meat may have released as it cooked. Press the **Cancel** button to turn off the Instant Pot.

Garnish the kheema with the cilantro. Serve it warm in the pav with onion, jalapeño (if using) and lime wedges.

Variations

• You can use any kind of minced meat: chicken thighs, lamb, beef or pork.

• Make the kheema vegetarian by using crumbled paneer or vegan by using crumbled tofu instead of ground meat. Decrease the cooking time to 5 minutes.

Sweet Endings

I don't have much of a sweet tooth, but I do indulge in sweet treats every once in a while. However, I am surrounded by family and friends who absolutely love desserts, and I love to create sweet endings for the festive meals and get-togethers I enjoy with them.

It wasn't until after I went to culinary school that I gained confidence in whipping up elegant desserts. I learned quite a few French desserts in school and experimented at home, putting little Indian touches on them, like the Rabdi Pots de Crème (Cardamom- and Rose-Scented Cream Custards; page 144) or the Khubani Clafoutis (Dried Apricot Clafoutis; page 158).

I like the Instant Pot for making desserts because it is faster than baking in the oven—there is no preheating required. It's also more efficient and less time-consuming for some traditional Indian dessert recipes that need hours of simmering and stirring on the stove.

Every now and then, I make some of the very traditional Indian desserts with nontraditional ingredients, like the Pumpkin Spice Sheera (Semolina Porridge; page 156), made with pumpkin puree and scented with pumpkin spice. I infuse the classic phirni with my favorite chocolate-fruit pairing to make Chocolate-Orange Phirni (Ground Rice and Milk Pudding; page 155). I adore the Bengali classic, which I turn into Maple–Brown Sugar Mishti Doi (Sweetened Yogurt; page 141). The Mithai Cake (Rose-Scented Almond and Pistachio Cake with Saffron Icing; page 138) is an ultimate creation of mine that brings together all the flavors of traditional Indian sweets into one soft and light cake!

In this chapter, I also wanted to include some of my childhood favorites, like the Amba Badam Burfi (Mango and Almond Fudge; page 148) and an all-time favorite, the Basundi (Milk Pudding; page 152), for which the Instant Pot is a game changer with its slow-cook functionality! In addition, I have also included a couple of my mom's signature concoctions that I have updated and retrofitted to the Instant Pot, like the Bread Ka Meetha (Bread Pudding; page 151) and the Doodhi Halwa (Bottle Gourd Pudding; page 147).

Mithai Cake

(Rose-Scented Almond and Pistachio Cake with Saffron Icing)

Traditional Indian sweets and desserts are known as mithai in India, and they range from little squares of burfis (page 148) to hearty halwas (page 147). All of the mithai in India is made with a combination of a few key ingredients like saffron, almonds, pistachios and rose water. These ingredients were the inspiration for this cake, which brings all of those wonderful flavors together and transforms a basic cake made with eggs, butter, sugar and flour into a rich and decadent Indian mithai cake.

The icing for the cake is inspired by a traditional Maharashtrian yogurt-based dessert called shrikhand. I recommend using a good-quality saffron—Kashmiri saffron is perfect if you can find it—to get the natural golden-yellow hue!

Serves 8 to 12

Mithai Cake

Cooking spray or neutral oil of choice (see Notes)

1½ cups (188 g) all-purpose flour

½ cup (48 g) blanched almond flour (preferably superfine; see Notes)

1 tsp baking powder

1 tsp baking soda

¼ tsp salt

1 cup (200 g) granulated sugar

1 cup (240 ml) plain, unsweetened Greek yogurt, at room temperature

½ cup (114 g) unsalted butter, softened at room temperature

1 large egg, at room temperature

2 tbsp (30 ml) rose water

½ cup (62 g) raw pistachios, roughly chopped

1 cup (240 ml) water

To prepare the mithai cake, generously grease a 6-cup (1.4-L) Bundt® pan with cooking spray. Alternatively, brush the pan with oil. Set the Bundt pan aside. If you don't have a 6-cup (1.4-L) Bundt pan, you can use a round cake pan that is 7 inches (18 cm) in diameter.

Prepare an aluminum foil sling for conveniently transferring the cake pan in and out of the Instant Pot. Measure a 2½-foot (75-cm)-long piece of foil and fold it in half along its length, and then fold it in half once again. Set the foil aside.

In a medium bowl, whisk together the all-purpose flour, almond flour, baking powder, baking soda and salt. For a lighter and fluffier cake, spoon the flour into your measuring cup and gently level it with the back of a knife as opposed to scooping it out of the container with the measuring cup.

In a large bowl, use a hand mixer to beat together the granulated sugar, Greek yogurt, butter, egg and rose water until the ingredients are smooth.

Add the flour mixture to the sugar-yogurt mixture in two batches, one half at a time. After each addition, turn the hand mixer to low speed and mix the ingredients well to form a smooth, thick cake batter.

Using a spatula, gently fold the pistachios into the batter until everything is well combined.

Transfer the batter to the prepared Bundt pan. Cover the pan with a paper towel, then place a piece of aluminum foil over the paper towel. The foil should be secured well but should be loose and not sealed tightly. Place the covered pan on the foil sling. Bring the two ends of the sling together, over the top of the pan and scrunch them gently to secure them in place.

(continued)

Mithai Cake *(continued)*

Saffron Icing

¼ cup (60 ml) warm milk

½ tsp Kashmiri saffron threads

1 cup (120 g) powdered sugar

4 oz (112 g) cream cheese, at room temperature

Notes:

- You can substitute almond flour with almond meal, made from raw un-peeled almonds, or cashew flour. If you don't have almond flour, you can use all-purpose flour instead.

- Brushing the Bundt pan with oil or using cooking spray works better than greasing it with butter, as the milk solids in butter can act like glue, causing the batter to stick and making it difficult for the cake to come out of the pan.

Place the inner pot in the Instant Pot and pour in the water. Place the trivet in the bottom of the pot. Using the sling, lower the cake pan gently into the pot.

Close the Instant Pot's lid and turn the steam-release valve to the sealing position. Press the **Manual/Pressure Cook** button and set the timer for 35 minutes at **high pressure**.

While the cake bakes, prepare the saffron icing. Place the warm milk in a small bowl and add the Kashmiri saffron threads. Allow the saffron threads to soak in the milk while the cake bakes.

When the baking is complete, allow the pressure to release naturally—which will take 20 to 22 minutes—and then open the lid. Take the pan out of the pot and transfer it to a cooling rack. Let the cake sit, undisturbed, for 5 minutes. Open the foil sling, remove the foil on top of the pan and gently peel off the paper towel. Let the cake cool for 25 to 30 minutes.

While the cake cools, finish preparing the saffron icing. Do not strain the Kashmiri saffron threads from the milk. In a medium bowl, whisk together the saffron-infused milk, powdered sugar and cream cheese until the icing is smooth.

When the cake is cool enough to handle, invert the pan over a serving plate or a cake stand and lift the pan to remove the cake. Pour the desired amount of the icing over the cake, making sure it's fully covered. Slice the cake and serve it with any leftover icing on the side.

Maple–Brown Sugar Mishti Doi

(Sweetened Yogurt)

I'm a huge fan of Kankana Saxena, a fellow food blogger from the Bay Area who wrote the foreword for this book. Her cookbook, Taste of Eastern India, *is absolutely amazing! Her Instagram page and her YouTube channel are full of tempting pictures and videos. I've tried quite a few of her recipes, but the one that I found myself going back to over and over was the mishti doi, traditional Bengali sweetened yogurt. She has an easy-to-follow, detailed recipe and an elegant video published on her blog, playfulcooking.com.*

This recipe is an adaptation of Kankana's original recipe. Aside from making it entirely in the Instant Pot, I added my individual touch by swapping sugar and caramel sauce with maple sugar and maple syrup respectively.

Serves 6

Yogurt

1 cup (240 ml) plain, unsweetened Greek yogurt

2 cups (480 ml) whole milk (see Notes)

1 cup (240 ml) heavy cream

2 tbsp (30 ml) pure maple syrup, plus more for serving

1 cup (240 ml) water

Caramel Base

¼ cup (60 ml) water

½ cup (100 g) maple sugar (see Notes)

To prepare the yogurt, place the Greek yogurt in a strainer lined with cheesecloth or muslin. Bring the ends of the cheesecloth together and give the cheesecloth a tight squeeze to remove as much water as you can from the yogurt. Let the wrapped yogurt sit in the strainer while you prepare the rest of the recipe.

In a large measuring cup, combine the milk and heavy cream. Set the measuring cup aside.

To make the caramel base, place the inner pot in the Instant Pot and place the water and sugar in it. Stir well to combine the ingredients.

Close the Instant Pot's lid and turn the steam-release valve to the sealing position. Press the **Porridge** button and set the timer for 15 minutes at **high pressure**. When the cooking is complete, open the lid using a quick pressure release to depressurize the Instant Pot.

Press the **Cancel** button, and then press the **Sauté** button to make the yogurt base. Slowly pour ¼ cup (60 ml) of the milk–heavy cream mixture into the caramel base and stir well to combine the ingredients. Pour in another ¼ cup (60 ml) of the milk–heavy cream mixture and stir. Slowly pour in the remaining 2½ cups (600 ml) of the milk–heavy cream mixture, then add the maple syrup. Let the mixture come to a rolling boil, which will take 5 to 6 minutes. Stir it continuously, so that the milk doesn't stick to the bottom of the pot and burn.

Once the mixture is boiling, press the **Cancel** button. Let the mixture continue to boil and then simmer over the Instants Pot's residual heat for 5 minutes, stirring it continuously.

(continued)

Doodhi Halwa

(Bottle Gourd Pudding)

Bottle gourd or opo squash is just glorious in this traditional Indian dessert! My recipe is faster and lighter because I pressure-cook the gourd in its own juices along with the sugar and almond flour, and then I finish it off with a little cream. Also, I like to use almond flour instead of milk powder or the more commonly used khoya (dried evaporated milk solids). I love the nuttiness of the almond flour, which cannot be replicated with milk products.

Serves 6

2 tbsp (28 g) ghee (see Variations)

1 (3-lb [1.4-kg]) bottle gourd, ends trimmed, peeled, cored and grated (see Variations)

1 cup (200 g) granulated sugar

1 cup (95 g) blanched almond flour (preferably superfine; see Variations)

½ tsp ground cardamom

⅛ tsp salt

¼ cup (60 ml) heavy cream

1 tbsp (8 g) unsalted roasted pistachios, roughly chopped, for garnishing

1 tbsp (7 g) toasted slivered almonds, for garnishing

Edible rose petals, for garnishing (optional)

Edible gold or silver leaves, for garnishing (optional)

Place the inner pot in the Instant Pot and press the **Sauté** button. When the display reads "Hot," add the ghee and allow it to melt. Add the bottle gourd. Sauté the bottle gourd for 5 minutes to allow it to soften, stirring it frequently. Press the **Cancel** button to turn off the Instant Pot.

Add the sugar and almond flour and stir to combine everything well. Close the Instant Pot's lid and turn the steam-release valve to the sealing position. Press the **Porridge** button and set the timer for 5 minutes at **high pressure**. When the cooking is complete, open the lid using a quick pressure release to depressurize the Instant Pot. Press the **Cancel** button and add the cardamom and salt. Stir the ingredients to combine them well.

Press the **Sauté** button and sauté the mixture for 5 minutes, stirring it continuously to ensure nothing sticks to the bottom of the pot. Press the **Cancel** button and pour in the heavy cream. Stir to thoroughly combine the cream with the pudding.

Serve the pudding warm, or chill it in the refrigerator for at least 4 hours and serve it chilled. Garnish the pudding with the pistachios, almonds, rose petals (if using) and edible gold leaves (if using).

Variations

• Make the pudding vegan by replacing the ghee with coconut oil and the heavy cream with coconut cream.

• You can substitute the bottle gourd with 3 pounds (1.4 kg) of zucchini. Use the same settings for pressure and time.

• Make gajar halwa by substituting the gourd with 3 pounds (1.4 kg) of carrots and adding ½ cup (120 ml) of milk or water with the sugar and almond flour. Increase the cooking time to 10 minutes.

• Make the dish nut-free by swapping the almond flour with the same amount of milk powder and garnishing the pudding with only the rose petals and edible gold or silver leaves.

Amba Badam Burfi

(Mango and Almond Fudge)

Burfis are festive Indian sweet treats that have a fudge-like texture. They are infused with spices like cardamom or saffron, enriched with nuts like cashews, pistachios or almonds and flavored with fruits like mangoes, figs or dates. I tend to make mango-almond burfi often, since my pantry is always stocked with almond flour for baking and canned Alphonso mango pulp for making mango lassi.

The Instant Pot makes this burfi easy and takes away the guesswork for making the one-string-consistency sugar syrup that's necessary for the base of the burfi.

Makes 12 to 15 squares

¼ cup (60 ml) water

½ cup (100 g) granulated sugar

1 tsp ghee

¼ cup (60 ml) Alphonso mango pulp (see Note)

2 cups (190 g) blanched almond flour (preferably superfine), almond meal or cashew flour

¼ tsp ground cardamom

1 tbsp (8 g) raw pistachios, crushed, for garnishing

Edible silver leaves, for garnishing (optional)

Note:
Canned Alphonso mango pulp is readily available in Indian stores. You can also use puree made from fresh or frozen mangoes. Use exactly the quantity specified in the recipe to ensure a firm fudge.

Place the inner pot in the Instant Pot. In the pot, combine the water and sugar. Stir well to combine the two.

Close the Instant Pot's lid and turn the steam-release valve to the sealing position. Press the **Porridge** button and set the timer for 10 minutes at **high pressure**. When the cooking is complete, open the lid using a quick pressure release to depressurize the Instant Pot.

Stir in the ghee, mango pulp, almond flour and cardamom. Mix the ingredients well.

Press the **Sauté** button, then press the **Adjust** button to set the **Sauté** function to the **Less** setting. If you don't adjust the intensity of the **Sauté** function to **Less**, the mixture will cook unevenly and might even burn. Cook the mixture for 7 to 8 minutes, stirring it continuously, until it loses most of its moisture and comes together into a cohesive mass.

Press the **Cancel** button to turn off the Instant Pot.

Using kitchen mitts, carefully remove the inner pot and set it on the counter to stop the cooking process. Using a flexible spatula, press the mixture against the sides of the inner pot and gently knead the mixture with the spatula for 1 to 2 minutes to bring it together into a roughly shaped dough ball.

Place a large piece of parchment paper next to the inner pot. Transfer the dough to the parchment paper and place another large piece of parchment paper on top of it. Using a rolling pin, roll out the dough until it is ¼ inch (6 mm) thick. Remove the top piece of parchment paper. Let the dough rest for about 10 minutes.

Using a pizza cutter or a sharp knife, cut the dough into 1½- to 2-inch (4- to 5-cm) squares. Gently press the pistachios and silver leaves (if using) into the top of each square. The burfi squares will firm up as they cool. Store them in an airtight container on the counter for up to 2 days or in the refrigerator for up to 1 week.

Bread Ka Meetha

(Bread Pudding)

I remember Mom whipping up this luscious Indian bread pudding quite often as I was growing up. It is a specialty of Hyderabad, the capital of the southern state Telangana, where most of my dad's side of the family is from and still resides.

While most recipes require deep-frying the bread, this recipe calls for simply sautéing nuts and crumbled bread in some ghee until the mixture gets crispy and golden brown. After stirring in sugar and milk, it is steamed in the Instant Pot so that the bread soaks up all the milk. Serve this sprinkled with nuts or even à la mode!

Serves 6 to 8

6 tbsp (84 g) ghee, divided

3 to 4 pods green cardamom, seeds removed and lightly crushed

3 tbsp (27 g) raw almonds, roughly chopped

3 tbsp (27 g) raw cashews, whole or halved

3 tbsp (24 g) raw pistachios, roughly chopped

2 tbsp (28 g) walnuts, roughly chopped

1 (14-oz [392-g]) brioche bread or bread of choice, diced or crumbled (see Notes)

½ cup (100 g) granulated sugar (see Note)

¼ tsp ground nutmeg

1 cup (240 ml) milk

1 cup (240 ml) heavy cream

Place the inner pot in the Instant Pot and press the **Sauté** button. When the display reads "Hot," add 2 tablespoons (28 g) of the ghee and allow it to melt. Add the cardamom seeds. Let the seeds sizzle for about 30 seconds, and then add the almonds, cashews, pistachios and walnuts. Sauté the mixture for 3 to 4 minutes, stirring it frequently, until the nuts are light brown. Using a slotted spoon, transfer the nuts to a small bowl. Set the bowl aside.

Melt the remaining 4 tablespoons (56 g) of ghee in the inner pot. Add the bread. Toast the bread for 8 to 10 minutes, stirring it continuously, until it's fragrant and light golden brown in color. Press the **Cancel** button.

Add the sugar and nutmeg and stir to combine them well with the bread. Pour in the milk and heavy cream. Add half of the fried nuts and reserve the remaining nuts for garnishing the bread pudding.

Combine the ingredients well and close the Instant Pot's lid. Turn the steam-release valve to the sealing position. Press the **Steam** button and set the timer for 5 minutes at **low pressure**. When the cooking is complete, let the pressure release naturally for 10 minutes and then open the lid using a quick pressure release to finish depressurizing the Instant Pot.

Don't worry if the bottom of the pot appears to be slightly burnt after opening the lid. Stir the bread pudding well with a wooden spoon, scraping the bottom of the pot to loosen any toasted bits.

Spoon the bread pudding into bowls and garnish each serving with the reserved fried nuts. Serve the bread pudding immediately.

Note: The quantity of sugar used is based on the type of bread. Brioche bread is already sweet, and the quantity of sugar has been adjusted for it. If you use a bread that is not sweet or prefer your desserts on the sweeter side, increase the amount of sugar to the desired level.

Basundi

(Milk Pudding)

This smooth, creamy milk-based dessert is from my home state of Maharashtra and is a simple dish made by boiling and then reducing cardamom- and nutmeg-scented sweetened milk over low heat for a while. The reduced milk is then chilled for a few hours before being garnished with saffron threads and charoli or chironji, lentil-sized, almond-flavored seeds that are commonly used in Indian sweets and that possess a texture similar to pine nuts.

Given that basundi is one of my favorite Indian desserts and not very popular or easily available, I make it at home quite often, thanks to the Instant Pot. I just dump all of the ingredients in the pot, and then it's ready to be chilled after slow-cooking overnight!

Serves 10 to 12

8 cups (1.9 L) whole milk

1 (14-oz [420-ml]) can sweetened condensed milk

¼ tsp ground cardamom

⅛ tsp ground nutmeg

Charoli (chironji), for garnishing

Kashmiri saffron threads, for garnishing

Edible flowers (such as nasturtium, chrysanthemum or marigold), for garnishing (optional)

Rinse the inside of the inner pot with cold tap water and drain it. Do not wipe the pot dry. This is an important step in preventing the milk solids from sticking to the bottom of the pot.

Pour the whole milk and sweetened condensed milk into the pot. Stir to combine them well, making sure the condensed milk has completely dissolved in the whole milk. Add the cardamom and nutmeg and stir the ingredients well to combine them.

Close the Instant Pot's lid. The pressure valve can be in either the venting or the sealing position. Press the **Slow Cook** button. Leave the setting on **Normal** and press the "**+**" button to set the timer for 8 hours.

After the slow-cooking is complete, press the **Cancel** button. Open the lid. You will find a thick skin of cream floating on top. Do not disturb it at this time.

Remove the inner pot from the Instant Pot. Let the inner pot sit on the counter until the milk pudding has come to room temperature. This should take about 2 hours. Once the milk pudding has cooled, you can either mix the thick cream skin on top into the pudding by stirring and breaking it with a spoon, or you can take the cream skin out and discard it.

Chill the pudding for at least 2 hours before serving it.

Spoon the chilled pudding into dessert bowls and garnish each serving with the charoli, Kashmiri saffron threads and edible flowers (if using).

Chocolate-Orange Phirni
(Ground Rice and Milk Pudding)

Phirni is the North Indian version of the popular Indian rice pudding, kheer, and is made with coarsely ground rice as opposed to the whole rice used for the latter. Its luscious and velvety texture comes from cooking the sweetened ground rice and milk mixture over low heat, so that the rice absorbs the milk as it cooks and turns thick and creamy. The Instant Pot's Porridge function works perfectly for this. I put my spin on the classic recipe by infusing it with an iconic flavor pairing—chocolate and orange. The two contrasting flavors create a magical experience for your palate!

Serves 12

⅓ cup (67 g) uncooked basmati rice

2 cups (480 ml) milk, divided

¼ cup (60 ml) water

1½ cups (360 ml) heavy cream

½ cup (100 g) sugar

¼ tsp salt

1 medium orange (see Variations)

½ cup (84 g) dark chocolate chips (see Variations)

Toasted walnut pieces, for garnishing

Candied orange peel, for garnishing (optional; see Variations)

Variation
• Make the classic phirni by adding ¼ teaspoon of ground cardamom and ¼ teaspoon of Kashmiri saffron threads along with the sugar and salt. Do not use the chocolate chips and the orange.

In a small bowl, soak the rice in ½ cup (120 ml) of the milk for about 30 minutes. Transfer the rice and milk to a food grinder or mini food processor. Pulse 4 or 5 times, until most of the rice is coarsely ground.

Place the inner pot in the Instant Pot and press the **Sauté** button. Pour in the water and let it start steaming. This should take about 2 minutes. This is key to prevent the milk from scorching and sticking to the bottom of the pot.

Press the **Cancel** button and pour in the ground rice and milk mixture. Pour in the remaining 1½ cups (360 ml) of milk and the heavy cream. Stir in the sugar. Sprinkle the salt and zest the orange directly over the pot. Stir the ingredients to combine them.

Close the Instant Pot's lid and turn the steam-release valve to the sealing position. Press the **Porridge** button and set the timer for 10 minutes at **high pressure**. When the cooking is complete, allow the pressure to release naturally—which will take 15 to 20 minutes—and then open the lid.

Press the **Cancel** button. Stir in the chocolate chips. The chocolate chips will start melting right away in the hot rice and milk porridge. Close the lid and let the pudding rest for 2 hours to allow it to thicken and cool. You can speed up the cooling process by leaving the lid open and stirring the pudding occasionally. Once it's close to room temperature, squeeze in the juice from half of the orange and stir. Taste and add more orange juice, if desired.

Spoon the pudding into ⅓-cup (80-ml)-sized serving bowls and chill the pudding in the refrigerator for at least 2 hours.

Garnish the pudding with the toasted walnuts and candied orange peel (if using) before serving it.

Variation
• Substitute chocolate chips and orange with mango pulp to make mango phirni. Do not add the mango pulp right after opening the Instant Pot's lid; rather, stir it in when the pudding has cooled and is close to room temperature to prevent the milk from curdling.

Pumpkin Spice Sheera

(Semolina Porridge)

Sheera is the most common sweet offering made for religious festivities and prayers in Maharashtrian households. Even today, my mom quickly whips it up for holidays or for impromptu celebrations. Growing up, I had the sheera with sliced bananas or chunks of pineapple mixed in. During the mango season, Mom made mango sheera with mango pulp or chunks of mango mixed in.

Inspired by the seasonal fall flavors here in the United States, I love to make sheera with pumpkin puree and infuse it with the classic American pumpkin spice. This Instant Pot recipe is certainly more efficient than the traditional version, as it doesn't need the milk-water mixture to be boiled separately. It's just added to the pot with the semolina and steamed together.

Serves 4 to 6

¾ cup (170 g) ghee or butter or
¾ cup (180 ml) neutral oil of choice

1 cup (180 g) rava/sooji (coarse semolina)

1 cup (245 g) canned pumpkin puree (see Variation)

¾ cup (165 g) packed light brown sugar

1 tsp pumpkin spice (see Note)

1 cup (240 ml) water

2 cups (480 ml) whole milk

Toasted or candied pecans, for garnishing

Note: You can make your own pumpkin pie spice by mixing together ¼ teaspoon of ground cinnamon, 1 teaspoon of ground ginger, 1 teaspoon of ground cloves and 1 teaspoon of ground nutmeg.

Place the inner pot in the Instant Pot and press the **Sauté** button. When the display reads "Hot," add the ghee and allow it to melt. Add the semolina. Toast the semolina for 4 to 5 minutes, stirring it continuously, until it's fragrant and light golden brown in color.

Add the pumpkin puree and stir the ingredients to combine them well. Sauté the mixture for 2 to 3 minutes, stirring it continuously, until the pumpkin puree is completely incorporated and the ghee separates out.

Press the **Cancel** button to turn off the Instant Pot.

Add the brown sugar and pumpkin spice and stir to combine the ingredients.

Pour in the water and milk. Stir to combine everything well. Deglaze the bottom of the pot by scraping it with a wooden spoon. This is an important step; if the bottom of the pot is not deglazed well, the "burn" error might appear during the pressure-cooking stage.

Close the Instant Pot's lid and turn the steam-release valve to the sealing position. Press the **Steam** button and adjust the timer to 3 minutes at **low pressure**. When the cooking is complete, allow the pressure to release naturally—which will take 15 to 20 minutes—and then open the lid. Don't worry if there is a little moisture and the bottom of the pot appears to be slightly burnt after opening the lid. Stir the porridge well while scraping the bottom of the pot with a wooden spoon.

Transfer the porridge to individual serving bowls and garnish each serving with the pecans. Serve the porridge warm or at room temperature.

Variation

You can substitute pumpkin puree with mango puree and the pumpkin spice with ground cardamom to make mango sheera.

Khubani Clafoutis

(Dried Apricot Clafoutis)

Light, not-too-sweet and bursting with a juicy surprise in every bite, this elegant French dessert is something I learned to make in my very first class at culinary school. Traditionally made with black cherries mixed in a cake-like batter, clafouti looks and feels like a soft and moist but dense cake. You'll find a lot of variations made with different berries, apricots, peaches and even apples or pears. Surprisingly, this dessert turns out lighter when made in the Instant Pot rather than the oven.

I put an Indian spin on the classic by making it with khubani, a traditional Kashmiri dessert made by soaking dried apricots in a sugar syrup that is infused with cinnamon, cardamom and ginger.

Serves 6

Clafoutis

¾ cup (94 g) all-purpose flour

¾ cup (150 g) plus 3 tbsp (45 g) granulated sugar, divided

½ tsp ground cardamom

2 large eggs

½ cup (120 ml) milk

½ cup (120 ml) heavy cream

4½ tsp (18 g) butter, softened

Sliced almonds, as needed (optional)

Powdered sugar, for garnishing

Khubani

18 to 20 dried apricots, quartered

1¾ cups (420 ml) water, divided

1 to 2 pods green cardamom, lightly crushed

1-inch (2.5-cm) piece cinnamon bark

½-inch (1.3-cm) piece fresh ginger, quartered lengthwise

2 tbsp (30 g) granulated sugar

Start by making the clafoutis' batter, as it will need to rest. In a medium bowl, combine the flour, ¾ cup (150 g) of the granulated sugar and ground cardamom. Set the flour mixture aside.

In another small bowl, whisk together the eggs, milk and heavy cream until they are well blended. Pour the milk mixture into the flour mixture and whisk them together until they form a smooth batter. Let the batter rest for 30 to 60 minutes.

While the batter rests, make the khubani. Place the inner pot in the Instant Pot. In the inner pot, combine the apricots, ¾ cup (180 ml) of the water, crushed cardamom pods, cinnamon bark and ginger. Sprinkle the granulated sugar over the mixture and stir to combine everything.

Close the Instant Pot's lid and turn the steam-release valve to the sealing position. Press the **Manual/Pressure Cook** button and set the timer for 5 minutes at **high pressure**. When the cooking is complete, allow the pressure to release naturally—which will take 12 to 15 minutes—and then open the lid.

Press the **Cancel** button. Open the lid and discard the ginger, cardamom pods and cinnamon bark. Drain the apricots and set them aside (see Note).

Rinse the inner pot clean and set it aside.

To make the clafoutis, grease each of 6 (½-cup [120-ml]) ramekins with ¾ teaspoon of the butter and dust them with the remaining 3 tablespoons (45 g) of granulated sugar.

Arrange the rehydrated apricots in an even layer at the bottom of each of the ramekins. Divide the prepared batter among the ramekins equally. Top the batter with the almonds (if using).

Place the inner pot in the Instant Pot and add the remaining 1 cup (240 ml) of water to the pot. Place the trivet in the pot and set 3 ramekins on it. Place another trivet over the ramekins, and then set the remaining three ramekins on the second trivet. If you do not have two trivets, make the clafoutis in two batches.

Close the Instant Pot's lid and turn the steam-release valve to the venting position. Press the **Steam** button and set the timer for 15 minutes at **high pressure**. Set a kitchen timer for the same amount of time, because with the steam-release valve in the venting position, the Instant Pot timer does not work accurately as the pressure doesn't get a chance to build up in the process.

After the steaming is complete, press the **Cancel** button. Allow any developed pressure to release naturally and the pressure valve to drop, which will take 1 to 2 minutes.

Open the lid and, using kitchen mitts, carefully take the ramekins out of the Instant Pot. Let them cool for about 2 minutes. Sprinkle them with the powdered sugar, then serve them immediately.

Alternatively, you can top the steamed ramekins with a little more granulated sugar and caramelize it with a culinary torch or broil it in the oven for 2 to 3 minutes to form a crispy, hard top like that of a crème brûlée. Serve the clafoutis immediately.

*See photo on page 136.

Note:
You can reserve the apricot liquid for flavoring teas, cocktails or other drinks.

Lip-Smacking Relishes

Condiments are a must on the Indian dining table! When I was growing up—and even now when she's in charge of the kitchen—Mom ensures that there is a lip-smacking relish in the top left-hand corner of our plates, be it a pickle, some sort of preserves or a chutney. Naturally, I'm wired to do the same!

In this chapter, I'm sharing Instant Pot versions of a few of the relishes that I tend to make over and over again. I used to make all of these on the stove—but because they need to be simmered for a while, I converted them to the Instant Pot. That way, I don't need to babysit the pot and can get consistent results with precise cooking times. Take the Szechuan Chutney (Chili-Garlic Sauce; page 168) as an example. It is something you will always find in my refrigerator—but homemade, not from the store! I make a big batch quickly in the Instant Pot and it stays good for months.

In the fall season, when the green apple tree in my yard is laden with fruit, I have to make the Chhundo (Green Apple Relish; page 166). I love to smear it on some crostini with goat or Brie cheese and serve it as an elegant appetizer for Thanksgiving dinner.

With one Maharashtrian (that would be me) and one South Indian (that would be my husband) in the house, traditional condiments like Kolambiche Lonche (Shrimp Pickle; page 162) from my home state and Tomato Pachadi (Curry Leaf–Scented Chunky Tomato Sauce; page 165) from his make frequent appearances on our dining table, especially to accompany some of the typical main courses from each of our native cuisines.

While you can find a few traditional pickle and relish recipes on my website, the condiments included in this chapter are more of the instant kind: quick to make and gone in no time!

Kolambiche Lonche

(Shrimp Pickle)

This traditional Maharashtrian shrimp pickle is a little tangy and deliciously spicy. It's pretty easy to make and is always a huge hit at the dining table. While there are many recipes that call for resting the pickle for a day or two, this version can be had freshly prepared, since pressure-cooking in the Instant Pot develops its flavor instantaneously.

I like to make the pickle masala from scratch using some basic and easily available spices. It definitely makes a difference and gives this lip-smacking shrimp pickle a wonderful flavor that is perfect with simple steamed rice, plain dal (varan) or on the side of some warm Masale Bhaat (Spiced Rice Pilaf; page 100).

Makes 2 cups (350 g)

Marinade

8 oz (224 g) small shrimp, peeled, deveined and tails removed

½-inch (1.3-cm) piece fresh ginger, finely grated

2 cloves garlic, finely grated

½ tsp ground turmeric

1 tbsp (6 g) Kashmiri red chili powder

1 tsp salt

Lonche Masala

2 tsp (6 g) mustard seeds

2 tsp (6 g) black peppercorns

2 tsp (8 g) methi (fenugreek) seeds

1 tsp ground turmeric

½ tsp asafetida

½ tsp cumin seeds

½ tsp coriander seeds

4 to 5 dried spicy red chilies (see Variation)

Pickle

¼ cup (60 ml) mustard oil or neutral oil of choice

1 tsp mustard seeds

¼ tsp asafetida

12 to 15 fresh curry leaves

1 tsp powdered jaggery or coconut palm sugar

Juice of ½ medium lemon or lime

Start by preparing the marinade. In a medium bowl, combine the shrimp, ginger, garlic, turmeric, Kashmiri red chili powder and salt. Toss the shrimp to coat them with the marinade. Set the bowl of shrimp aside.

To prepare the lonche masala, place the mustard seeds, peppercorns, methi seeds, turmeric, asafetida, cumin seeds, coriander seeds and red chilies in a spice grinder. Grind the ingredients to a fine powder.

To make the pickle, place the inner pot in the Instant Pot and press the **Sauté** button. When the display reads "Hot," add the mustard oil. When the oil starts shimmering, add the mustard seeds, asafetida and curry leaves. When the seeds sizzle and the curry leaves splutter, press the **Cancel** button.

Add the lonche masala and stir to combine it with the pickle. Let the ground spice mixture bloom in the hot oil over the Instant Pot's residual heat for about 2 minutes, stirring it continuously.

Transfer the marinated shrimp and the marinade to the spiced oil. Season with powdered jaggery and combine the ingredients well.

Close the Instant Pot's lid and turn the steam-release valve to the sealing position. Press the **Manual/Pressure Cook** button and set the timer for 2 minutes at **low pressure**. When the cooking is complete, allow the pressure to release naturally—which will take 10 to 12 minutes—and then open the lid.

Add the lemon juice to the pickle. Stir the pickle to combine everything well.

Let the shrimp pickle cool completely and serve it at room temperature. You can store it in an airtight container in the refrigerator for up to 3 days.

Variation

If you prefer less heat, use fewer dried chilies, or omit them entirely.

Tomato Pachadi

(Curry Leaf–Scented Chunky Tomato Sauce)

South Indian cuisine has a variety of fresh pickles known as pachadis. Pachadis are similar to chutneys or relishes made with raw or cooked vegetables and fruits, like pineapple, green mango, beets, eggplant, okra, gourds or leafy greens like gongura along with coconut or yogurt at times.

I make a big batch of this sweet and sour tomato pachadi by dumping everything in the Instant Pot and pressure-cooking it for a few minutes. It's great with Kanchipuram Idlis (Turmeric-Spiced Rice and Lentil Cakes; page 124), it works well as a topping with goat cheese or fresh mozzarella cheese on crostini and it's delicious smeared in a wrap or sandwich with grilled chicken!

Makes 2 cups (450 g)

2 tbsp (30 ml) neutral oil of choice

1 tsp mustard seeds

8 to 10 fresh curry leaves

2 to 3 whole dried spicy round or long red chilies (substitute Kashmiri dried red chilies for less heat)

1 small red onion, minced

Salt, as needed

4 to 5 cloves garlic, minced

½ tsp freshly ground black pepper

Red chili powder, as needed

1 tbsp (16 g) tomato paste

3 medium tomatoes, pureed (see Variations)

1 tsp powdered jaggery or coconut palm sugar

½ tsp tamarind concentrate

18 to 20 sprigs fresh cilantro, leaves roughly chopped

Place the inner pot in the Instant Pot and press the **Sauté** button. When the display reads "Hot," add the oil, mustard seeds, curry leaves and spicy red chilies. When the seeds sizzle and the curry leaves splutter, add the onion. Season the mixture with salt to help the onion soften. Sauté the mixture for 5 to 7 minutes, stirring it frequently, until the onion is translucent.

Stir in the garlic and sauté the mixture for 1 minute. Stir in the black pepper and red chili powder. Sauté the mixture for about 30 seconds to let the spices bloom, and then add the tomato paste and the pureed tomatoes. Season the mixture with the powdered jaggery and tamarind concentrate. Stir to combine the ingredients well. Taste the mixture and add additional salt if needed.

Cook the mixture for another 2 to 3 minutes, until the tomatoes lose most of their moisture. Press the **Cancel** button to turn off the Instant Pot. Add the cilantro and stir to combine the ingredients.

Close the Instant Pot's lid and turn the steam-release valve to the sealing position. Press the **Manual/Pressure Cook** button and set the timer for 5 minutes at **high pressure**. When the cooking is complete, allow the pressure to release naturally—which will take 12 to 15 minutes—and then open the lid.

Let the tomato pachadi cool completely, and serve it at room temperature. You can store it in an airtight container in the refrigerator for up to 2 weeks.

Variations

- Replace half or all of the tomatoes with diced eggplant to make eggplant pachadi. Add ¼ cup (60 ml) of water before adding the eggplant and make sure the pot is deglazed to avoid the "burn" error.

- Substitute the tomatoes with diced and peeled green mango to make mango pachadi. Skip the tamarind concentrate and use about ¼ cup (40 g) of powdered jaggery or coconut palm sugar, or however much is needed to balance the flavors.

Chhundo

(Green Apple Relish)

Chhundo is a sweet and spicy Indian relish that hails from the western state of Gujarat. It is traditionally made by cooking grated green mangoes with salt, sugar, jaggery and spices. With the bounty of green apples in my backyard, I experimented by using them to make chhundo one year, and it was a great success! Green apples are quite similar to green mangoes in texture and flavor and worked well in the recipe.

While this variation with green apple works perfectly in the classic pairing of chhundo and methi theplas (fenugreek flatbreads), I love to put it on an appetizer cheese board along with creamy Brie, buttery Gouda or tangy goat cheese and crackers or crostini.

Makes 2 cups (350 g)

3 medium green apples, washed, cored and grated (see Variation)

½ cup (80 g) powdered jaggery or coconut palm sugar

½ cup (100 g) granulated sugar

2 tsp (4 g) ground cumin

Red chili powder, as needed

1 tsp red pepper flakes

¾ tsp salt, or as needed

¼ cup (60 ml) water

Place the inner pot in the Instant Pot. Place the apples, powdered jaggery, granulated sugar, cumin, red chili powder, red pepper flakes, salt and water in the pot. Stir well to combine the ingredients.

Close the Instant Pot's lid and turn the steam-release valve to the sealing position. Press the **Manual/Pressure Cook** button and set the timer for 3 minutes at **high pressure**. When the cooking is complete, allow the pressure to release naturally—which will take 10 to 15 minutes—and then open the lid.

Press the **Cancel** button to turn off the Instant Pot. Let the cooked relish sit in the inner pot for about 2 hours, until it cools completely. The relish will thicken as it cools. Transfer the chhundo to an airtight glass jar and store it in the refrigerator. It should be good for about 3 months.

Variation

Make the classic version by substituting green apples with green mangoes. Adjust the amounts of jaggery and sugar to the desired level of sweetness.

Szechuan Chutney

(Chili-Garlic Sauce)

I bet you can tell from the name itself that this is a fusion recipe! It's a condiment from Indian-Chinese cuisine that's made with red chilies and garlic, is sweet and sour, not too hot but deliciously spicy. It's not just good as a condiment to spice up soups, like the Manchow Soup (Chicken and Vegetable Soup; page 55), but is also great as a base for classic dishes like the Szechuan Noodles (Spaghetti in Szechuan Sauce; page 45) or used as a marinade, like in my recipe for Drums of Heaven (Chicken Wings; page 127).

Szechuan chutney is available in Indian stores or online on Amazon, but it's quick and easy to make a big batch in the Instant Pot and store it in the refrigerator for months, like I do!

Makes 2 cups (256 g)

20 whole dried Kashmiri red chilies, stems removed

10 whole dried spicy red chilies, stems removed (see Variation)

2 cups (480 ml) water

25 large cloves garlic, smashed and peeled

3-inch (8-cm) piece fresh ginger, roughly chopped

½ medium rib celery, roughly chopped

2 medium green onions, roughly chopped

½ cup (120 ml) sesame oil or neutral oil of choice (see Notes)

2 tbsp (30 ml) soy sauce (see Notes)

½ cup (120 ml) ketchup

½ tsp black pepper

½ to 1 tsp salt

Place the inner pot in the Instant Pot. Place the Kashmiri red chilies, spicy red chilies and water in it. Be sure to thoroughly wash your hands after handling the chilies.

Close the Instant Pot's lid and turn the steam-release valve to the sealing position. Press the **Steam** button and adjust the timer for 5 minutes at **high pressure**. When the cooking is complete, allow the pressure to release naturally—which will take 15 to 17 minutes—and then open the lid. Be careful as you open the lid, because there will be spicy fumes from cooking the hot chilies.

Using a pair of tongs, transfer the cooked chilies to a blender. Transfer ¼ cup (60 ml) of the cooking liquid to the blender. Reserve the remaining cooking liquid in a medium bowl or measuring cup.

Let the chilies and cooking liquid cool for 2 minutes, and then blend them into a smooth paste.

In a food processor, combine the garlic, ginger, celery and green onions. Process the ingredients until they are finely chopped. If you do not have a food processor, make sure the ingredients are finely chopped or minced.

Rinse the inner pot and wipe it dry. Place it in the Instant Pot and press the **Sauté** button, then use the **Adjust** button to set **Sauté** to **Less**. If you don't adjust the intensity of the Sauté function to Less, the sesame oil and the garlic will burn on high heat and cause the sauce to taste bitter.

When the display reads "Hot," add the sesame oil. When the oil starts shimmering, add the chopped mixture of garlic, ginger, celery and green onions. Sauté the mixture for 8 to 10 minutes, stirring it frequently, until the raw smell of ginger and garlic goes away.

Stir in the ground chili paste and sauté the mixture for 5 to 7 minutes, until the oil separates out.

Press the **Cancel** button. Add ½ cup (120 ml) of the reserved cooking liquid and deglaze the bottom of the pot, in case there are burnt bits stuck at the bottom. This is an important step; if the bottom of the pot is not deglazed well, the "burn" error might appear during the pressure-cooking stage.

Stir in the soy sauce and the ketchup. Season the mixture with the black pepper and salt and mix everything together well.

Close the Instant Pot's lid and turn the steam-release valve to the sealing position. Press the **Manual/Pressure Cook** button and set the timer for 5 minutes at **low pressure**. When the cooking is complete, allow the pressure to release naturally—which will take 4 to 5 minutes—and then open the lid.

Press the **Cancel** button. Let the cooked sauce sit in the inner pot for about 2 hours, until it has cooled completely. The relish will thicken as it cools. Transfer it to an airtight glass jar and store it in the refrigerator. It should last for about 3 months.

Notes:

• Make sure to use the freshest sesame oil you can; otherwise, it can impart an unpleasant taste and smell to the sauce. If the oil smells stale or has a harsh aroma, it may have gone rancid and should be discarded.

• If you are using dark soy sauce, omit or adjust the amount of salt as needed.

Variation

If you prefer a milder chutney, substitute the dried spicy red chilies with Kashmiri red chilies.

*See photo on page 160.

Pantry Must-Haves and Staples

Indian food is fairly straightforward but gets its complex flavors from the use of a variety of spices that are the cornerstone of Indian cooking. Various spices are mixed together to create masalas, or spice blends.

In this chapter, I'm sharing a few hacks that I have developed to make small-batch masalas for use in specific recipes included in this book. There's the most commonly known and used Easy Garam Masala (Spice Blend Using Jarred Spices; page 172) that can be easily created by mixing ground jarred spices that you might have lying around in your kitchen cabinet. You can add a couple more ingredients to the Easy Garam Masala to make my Quick Goda Masala (Traditional Maharashtrian Spice Blend; page 175), which is unique to some of the Maharashtrian recipes that appear in the book. Lastly, you can make the traditional Rustic Kanda Lasun Masala (Onion-Garlic Spice Mix; page 176) that's not just a spice blend but also works like a dry chutney or a rub for many recipes beyond this book.

In addition to the recipes for the different spice blends, in this chapter I have included a recipe for Basic Raita (Salad with Spiced Yogurt Dressing; page 179), along with several ideas for variations, that can be served as an accompaniment to almost all of the main dishes included in the book.

Easy Garam Masala

(Spice Blend Using Jarred Spices)

I'm sure you have a bunch of ground spices in your cabinet that you may have bought for that one specific recipe—and then you got stuck with what's left over and don't know what else to do with it. If you're trying to figure out what you could do with all those spices you have lying around, I have an idea for how you can use up some of them: mix them up and make your own garam masala! This version is my quick formula. However, if you have a favorite brand of garam masala or have your own family recipe for it, by all means, use it in the recipes that call for it and save the individual spices for another time!

Makes ¼ cup (24 g)

1 tbsp (6 g) ground cumin
4½ tsp (9 g) ground coriander
1½ tsp (3 g) ground cardamom
1½ tsp (3 g) black pepper
1 tsp ground cinnamon
½ tsp ground cloves
½ tsp ground nutmeg

Place the cumin, coriander, cardamom, black pepper, cinnamon, cloves and nutmeg in a small, clean, airtight glass jar. Close the jar's lid and shake the jar well to combine the spices. Store the spice mixture in a cool, dry place away from direct sunlight for up to 6 months.

Quick Goda Masala

(Traditional Maharashtrian Spice Blend)

I use the classic Maharashtrian spice blend, goda (sweet) masala, a lot in my cooking, both at home in my kitchen and in quite a few recipes in this book. While you can find a detailed recipe for making the spice blend from scratch on my website, I'm sharing a hack that I came up with using my Easy Garam Masala (Spice Blend Using Jarred Spices; page 172) and a couple of other easily available key ingredients when I was out of the goda masala. It comes pretty close to the original!

If you can easily find goda masala in grocery stores near you or have your own family recipe for it, by all means, use it in the recipes that call for it.

Makes 3 tablespoons (18 g)

1 tbsp (6 g) Easy Garam Masala (page 172)

1 tbsp (6 g) desiccated coconut or unsweetened coconut flakes

1 tsp white sesame seeds

1 tsp red chili powder (see Variation)

¼ tsp ground turmeric

In a spice grinder, combine the Easy Garam Masala, coconut, sesame seeds, red chili powder and turmeric. Grind the ingredients until they are powdered and well combined. Store the goda masala spice blend in an airtight container in a cool, dark place for up to 6 months.

Variation
You can substitute half or all of the red chili powder with Kashmiri red chili powder.

Rustic Kanda Lasun Masala

(Onion-Garlic Spice Mix)

Kolhapur, one of the major cities of Maharashtra state, is the home for the super-hot kanda lasun masala. Unlike most Indian masalas, which have finely ground, powderlike consistencies, this unique spice blend is chunky, as it is made by roasting onions, garlic and dry red chilies along with an array of spices. With its coarse texture, similar to a dry garlic chutney, this masala is also served as a condiment with meals or sprinkled on toasted bread, hot parathas or plain yogurt to spice things up.

If you can easily find this masala in grocery stores near you, feel free to use it in the recipes that call for it, but note that it'll be a lot spicier!

Makes ⅔ cup (65 g)

1 tbsp (15 ml) neutral oil of choice

¼ tsp asafetida

4 to 5 medium Asian shallots, thickly sliced (see Notes)

4 to 5 cloves garlic, smashed and peeled

½-inch (1.3-cm) piece fresh ginger, roughly chopped

2 tbsp (16 g) unsweetened coconut flakes 2 tbsp (12 g) unsweetened shredded or desiccated coconut

5 to 6 dried spicy red chilies, stems removed and broken into smaller pieces (see Variation)

1 pod green cardamom, gently smashed open

2 to 3 whole cloves

8 to 10 black peppercorns

½-inch (1.3-cm) piece cinnamon bark

1 tsp coriander seeds

1 tsp cumin seeds

½ tsp sesame seeds

1 small dried bay leaf, torn into small pieces

1 tbsp (6 g) Kashmiri red chili powder (see Notes)

Salt, as needed

In a medium skillet over medium heat, warm the oil. When it starts shimmering, add the asafetida. When the asafetida froths, stir in the shallots, garlic, ginger, coconut, spicy red chilies, cardamom, cloves, peppercorns, cinnamon bark, coriander seeds, cumin seeds, sesame seeds and bay leaf.

Sauté the mixture for 8 to 10 minutes, stirring it frequently, until the shallots, garlic and coconut flakes are golden brown in color and the spices are fragrant. Turn off the heat and let the mixture cool completely in the skillet.

Transfer the cooled mixture to a spice grinder or a small food grinder. Add the Kashmiri red chili powder and the salt and pulse to grind the mixture to a coarse powder.

Transfer the masala to an airtight container and store it in a cool, dark place for up to 1 week or in the refrigerator for up to 1 month.

Notes:

• Asian shallots are similar to pearl red onions and easily available in Indian or Asian grocery stores. If you cannot find them, you can use the more common French shallots as a substitute.

• Kashmiri red chili powder is a key ingredient in this recipe. It is relatively mild in heat and gives the masala a vibrant red color. Mild Hungarian paprika is a good substitute if you can't find it.

Variation

Use fewer dried red chilies or discard their seeds for less heat.

Basic Raita

(Salad with Spiced Yogurt Dressing)

Raita is the quintessential Indian side salad made with diced onions, tomatoes and cucumbers tossed in a seasoned yogurt dressing, served primarily with rice dishes like pulaos or biryanis but also on the side to round off any meal.

While the basic recipe is made with either one or all of the three aforementioned vegetables, I like to make other versions using the same yogurt dressing as the base and toss in other vegetables along with the onions, like cooked beets or pumpkin, boiled potatoes, roasted bell peppers or spicy fried chickpea flour balls called boondi. You can also use fruits like pineapple, guava, apple, pomegranate and so on. In addition, you can play with the ratio of yogurt to vegetables.

Serves 4 to 6

Dressing

1 cup (240 ml) Greek yogurt

1 cup (240 ml) low-fat buttermilk

1 tsp ground cumin

Black Indian salt, as needed (see Notes)

½ tsp sugar

2 to 3 green bird's-eye chilies, thinly sliced (see Notes)

8 to 10 sprigs fresh cilantro, leaves roughly chopped

4 to 5 sprigs fresh mint, leaves roughly chopped (optional)

Salad

1 small onion, diced small

1 small tomato, diced small

1 mini cucumber or small Persian cucumber, finely diced

To make the dressing, whisk together the Greek yogurt, buttermilk, cumin, black Indian salt and sugar in a medium bowl until everything is well combined. Stir in the bird's-eye chilies, cilantro and mint (if using).

To make the salad, add the onion, tomato and cucumber to the dressing and mix everything together well. Refrigerate the raita until you are ready to serve it.

Notes:

• Black Indian salt, commonly known as kala namak, is widely available in Indian stores or on Amazon and other online retailers.

• If you prefer a milder flavor, you can use fewer chilies or omit them entirely. As another option, you can substitute the green chilies with red pepper flakes or red chili powder to suit your taste.

Essential Ingredients

Throughout this book, you'll find a few essential ingredients and ready-to-use products that are listed as serving suggestions or toppings for various recipes. This section provides brief information on those products. All of these items can be purchased at Indian grocery stores and some are also available online on Amazon.

Asafetida

This is the dried sap from the root of a perennial herb in the celery family. It's dull brown in color with an extremely pungent odor that turns into a pleasant onion-garlic flavor and aroma when it's added during cooking. It offers digestive and other health benefits and is indispensable in Indian cooking. There is no substitute. If you don't have it, skip it.

Black Salt

Black salt is a pungent-smelling rock salt that offers digestive health benefits. It is not black but light pinkish-gray in color and turns black when sprinkled over foods, imparting a pleasantly tangy flavor. It is not a replacement for table salt.

Chilies and Chili Powder

Fresh Indian green chilies are long, slender and bright green-yellow in color. They're not easily available and can be replaced with green bird's-eye chilies, which are also called Thai chilies. Dried red chilies are earthy, pretty spicy and can be either long or round in shape. Mexican chiles de árbol are excellent substitutes. Red chili powder—made by grinding the dried red chilies—is hot, has a deep red color and can be substituted with cayenne pepper.

Cinnamon Bark

Cinnamon bark is essentially cassia cinnamon from the Indian bay leaf and other cassia trees with loosely rolled, almost flat quills. It has a less sweet but intense aroma and a mildly bitter flavor. You can substitute it with the more commonly available, tightly rolled tubular cinnamon sticks.

Coconut and Coconut Milk

Coconut flesh is consumed in multiple ways in Indian cooking: fresh, dried or desiccated, grated, flaked or sliced and pulped into milk. One or all of these forms are easily available in not just Indian grocery stores but also in any regular supermarket.

Curry Leaves

These fresh leaves are small, oval or long paisley-shaped leaves of a small tree that is native to India. Lightly aromatic and slightly bitter in taste, they add a warm, exotic, mildly citrusy flavor when added to dishes. There is no substitute. If you don't have fresh curry leaves, skip them.

Edible Silver and Gold

These are superfine, micro-thin, weightless and extremely delicate foils made out of pure silver or gold. They are an integral part of Indian cuisine, used as garnishes for sweets and also for some savory dishes for better presentation.

Indian Breads

Naan, roti, parathas, Malabar parottas, bajri rotlas, appams and idiappams are just a few of the Indian breads that are suggested for serving with some of the main dishes included in this book. You can find them in the frozen section of Indian grocery stores.

Jaggery

This is the unrefined, natural product of sugarcane and has a golden-brown color. With its rich molasses content, it contains more nutrients than plain refined sugar. It adds complex sweetness with a hint of saltiness when used in cooking. It is available in the form of a powder or a block that can be grated or sliced.

Kashmiri Red Chilies and Kashmiri Red Chili Powder

These are mild, dark red or maroon chilies that are grown in Kashmir. They have a sweet aroma and a bitter aftertaste that mellows when added during cooking. The powder, which is essentially Indian paprika, is made by grinding dried chilies without any veins or seeds and imparts its brilliant red color to food without any heat. Mild Hungarian paprika is a great substitute.

Kashmiri Saffron

This is a tiny, thread-like spice derived from drying the stigmas of the saffron crocus flower that is primarily found in Kashmir. It has a warm and enticing fragrance. A pinch of saffron imparts a rich and exotic fragrance and a beautiful golden hue when added to dishes. Spanish saffron is a good substitute.

Kasuri Methi

Kasuri methi is air-dried fenugreek leaves that are used as a spice or a flavoring herb. It imparts a wonderful mellow aroma and a mild bitter flavor when added to foods. There is no substitute. If you don't have it, skip it.

Khus Khus (White Poppy Seeds)

These are tiny, pale, yellowish-white seeds with a light and sweet aroma and a nutty, almond-like flavor. They have a high protein content and offer digestive and other health benefits. You can use black or brown poppy seeds as a substitute for flavor, but note that they will impart their color to the food.

Kokum

Kokum is the sun-dried rind of the mangosteen fruit, the size of a cherry tomato, grown on the western coast of India and mainly used in Maharashtrian cooking to impart a sweet-sour flavor to food. It also adds a pretty purple-pink color that shows up best in paler sauces or curries.

Mango Pulp

Alphonso mango is the most popular variety of mango and is extensively grown in Ratnagiri, Maharashtra. It has the sweetest aroma and taste among all the mangoes and a beautiful, deep gold color. You can find a variety of brands of canned Alphonso mango pulp in Indian stores or on Amazon. Canned Kesar mango pulp is not the same as Alphonso, but it is a good substitute.

Ready-to-Use Masalas (Meat, Egg Curry, Rajma, Chhole, Biryani)

Everest brand masalas are the only ready-to-use masalas that I trust, since I grew up eating foods prepared with them. I use them in my cooking and also in some of the recipes in this book, and I highly recommend using them.

Rose Water and Edible Rose Petals

Rose water is essentially water that is infused with rose petals and has a strong, sweet, rosy fragrance and a delicate rose flavor. Dried edible rose petals and rose water are used in Indian cooking for a simple way to elevate both sweet and savory dishes.

Sev and Farsan

Sev are savory, deep-fried noodles of various shapes and sizes, ranging from thin to thick, made from chickpea flour batter and are either plain or seasoned with spices. Farsan is a mixture of chickpea noodles, peanuts, green peas, split peas and so on. They are used as garnishes or toppings for various chaat dishes (Indian street food).

Tamarind-Date Chutney

This is a sweet and sour sauce with a hint of heat and is served as a condiment with fried foods or savory pastries. It's also used for garnishing or topping classic Indian street-food dishes. It is available in the refrigerated section of Indian grocery stores. Shelf-stable tamarind chutneys are a good substitute.

Tamarind Concentrate

Tamarind concentrate looks like and has the consistency of balsamic reduction. It's thick, has an intensely tangy flavor and imparts a great depth of sour flavor when it's added to foods. Tamarind concentrate is very different from tamarind paste. Substitute 1 teaspoon of tamarind concentrate with 1 tablespoon (15 ml) of tamarind paste.